Gutsy Girls
Young Women Who Dare

Tina Schwager, P.T.A., A.T.,C.
and Michele Schuerger

Edited by Elizabeth Verdick

free spirit
PUBLiSHiNG®

Works
for kids™

Library of Congress Cataloging-in-Publication Data

Schwager, Tina, 1964–
    Gutsy girls : young women who dare / by Tina Schwager and Michele Schuerger ; edited by Elizabeth Verdick.
        p.   cm.
    Includes bibliographical references.
    Summary: Twenty-five young women share their adventures in such activities as skydiving, building homes, and mountain climbing, demonstrating the value of courage, commitment, and a positive attitude.
    ISBN 1-57542-059-7
    1. Young women—Case studies—Juvenile literature. 2. Women adventurers—Case studies—Juvenile literature. 3. Women athletes—Case studies—Juvenile literature. 4. Young women—Conduct of life—Juvenile literature. 5. Achievement motivation in women—Juvenile literature.   [1. Adventure and adventurers. 2. Women—Biography. 3. Conduct of life.] I. Schuerger, Michele, 1961–   . II. Title.
HQ129.S335   1999
155.5'33—dc21   98-52539
                                                                 CIP
                                                                 AC

Cover and interior design by Percolator
Cover photo Vianney Tisseau
Index prepared by Diana Witt
Author photos by Vicki Sears

The photo of Nahara Rodriguez on page 30 appears courtesy of Steven M. Falk/*Philadelphia Daily News;* the photo of Elizabeth Heaston on page 48 is produced by Vantine Studios, Hamilton, NY, and her photo on page 50 appears copyright Lynn Howlett Photography, Salem, OR; the photo of Rachel Cook on page 105 is used courtesy of Candid Color Photography; the photo of Diana Silbergeld on page 115 appears courtesy of Don Hagopian Photography; the photo of Leslee Olson on page 125 appears copyright Jeff Curtes/Burton Snowboards and her photo on page 129 is used courtesy of Vianney Tisseau; the photo of Lisa Taylor-Parisi on page 135 appears courtesy of Frank Molinski; and the photo of Veronica Kay on page 177 is used courtesy of John Keppler Photo.

NOTE: This book contains many recommendations for Web sites. Because Web sites change often and without notice, we can't promise every address listed will still be accurate when you read it. When in doubt, use a search engine.

---

10 9 8 7 6 5 4 3 2 1
Printed in the United States of America

Free Spirit Publishing Inc.
400 First Avenue North, Suite 616
Minneapolis, MN 55401-1724
(612) 338-2068
help4kids@freespirit.com
http://www.freespirit.com

Gutsy Girls is dedicated to every girl who has
dared to follow her dream—and especially
to the young women who share their remarkable
stories of courage and commitment in this book.
May you never lose sight of the endless
possibilities that await you, and may your
willing spirits continue to soar.

Acknowledgments

There's no way we could have gathered all of the information we needed to complete the stories for *Gutsy Girls* without the assistance of some wonderful individuals. It was great to discover how many helpful and enthusiastic people there are in this world, and we'd like to extend our thanks to them all.

First, we are deeply indebted to all of the moms, dads, siblings, friends, and supporters of these young women. Your enthusiasm for this project fueled our own excitement—we can't thank you enough for that.

Special thanks to all of our contacts who helped us research the stories: Marianne Higgins, Public Relations Specialist, U.S. Space and Rocket Center; Rob Mermin, founder and owner, Circus Smirkus; Robin Shallow, publicity department, *Sports Illustrated Women/Sport;* Cara D'Esopo, Susan Magrino Agency; Jamie Reno, Johnny Dodd, Beth Howard, and Dana Silbiger, freelance journalists; Chris Yager, Director, Where There Be Dragons; Brian Martin, Cohn and Wolfe; Amy Barrett, Burton Snowboards; Kim Drozd, Education Department, Maritime Aquarium at Norwalk; Michael Simpson, Racer and Corporate Programs, Frank Hawley's Drag Racing School; Dr. Steven Sroka and Russell J. Jacobson, Illinois State Geological Society; Mark Speckman, Head Football Coach, Willamette University; RoseMary Reed, Junior Competition Climbing Association; Marty Berger, Executive Director, Manhattan Island Foundation; Cliff Voliva, Willamette University; Bernard Anderson, American Bicycling Association; Leo Mehalic, Public Affairs Office, U.S. Naval Academy; Joe and Connie Pignatiello, Event and Media Coordinators for Susie Maroney's World Record Swim and owners of *Reel Lady;* Richard Batin, Batin's Kick Boxing; Mr. Eastburn, Assistant Principal, Widener Memorial; Trina Roth, chapter advisor, Alpha Chi Omega; Richard Budlong, Frank Molinski, Don Hagopian, Jeff Curtes, Steven Falk, Lynn Howlett,

John Keppler, and Vianney Tisseau, professional photographers; Kay Hafner, Girl Scouts of the U.S.A.; John Alderman, *Outside* magazine; and Carmelita Jordan, Habitat for Humanity.

A HUGE thanks to our family and friends for being understanding and hanging in there with us. We hope each of you knows how important you are and how much you are loved.

Our heartfelt appreciation goes to our editor, Elizabeth Verdick, for giving us this tremendous opportunity. We have enjoyed every second of it and look forward to working on many more rewarding projects with you.

And finally, to all of the remarkable young women who generously invited us into their lives, sharing their passions, fears, and personal victories—you are an inspiration. Your stories touched our hearts and helped remind us that people really can do anything if they set their minds to it. We hope your encouraging words and amazing deeds inspire girls and young women everywhere to follow their own dreams.

Contents

Merrick Johnston, Mountain Climber 6
She battled subzero temperatures, high altitudes, and frozen eyelashes. She also avoided a 3,000 foot fall into a crevasse and being
strangled by her own gear. Despite it all, Merrick triumphed to become the
youngest person to reach the top of Alaska's Mount McKinley, the highest peak in
North America.

Christy Hauptman, Skydiver 14
Thousands of feet above the earth, Christy takes a giant leap and
plummets out of a plane. Cool air rushes across her face as objects on
the ground increase in size; she pulls the parachute cord to slow her descent. The
thrill of skydiving is Christy's ultimate stress-reliever.

Carmella House, U.S. Naval Academy Midshipman ... 21
Carmella endured six grueling weeks of "yes, sirs," not speaking until
spoken to, military drills, sweat, and constant running to become a midshipman at the U.S. Naval Academy—one step closer to fulfilling her dream of being
an astronaut.

Nahara Rodriguez, Courage Award Winner 30
A car accident left her paralyzed from the waist down, but this hasn't
stopped Nahara from staying active and enjoying life to the fullest. She
swims and also plays wheelchair hockey and tennis. Her efforts in swimming
won her the Wilma Rudolph Courage Award, an honor that recognizes female athletes who have demonstrated amazing courage.

Introduction
You're Off to a Flying Start

If you could look into the heart of a gutsy girl, what do you think you'd see? Courage, determination, a boundless sense of adventure? Ambition, independence, a belief that dreams come true? Perhaps a passion for life; maybe a drive to blaze new trails or change the world? What's that spark inside her, igniting her desire to do the extraordinary?

The twenty-five young women you'll meet in this book have achieved amazing feats or faced unbelievable challenges. They weren't born with superhuman talents or strength. And they don't have any guarantee that they'll master each new activity they try. So why do they do it?

The young women profiled here are of various ages and have diverse backgrounds, but they share one common bond: *A deep love for what they do.* They love the feeling they get from it—joy, satisfaction, pride, an adrenaline rush. This fuels their desire to keep taking risks and to explore and reach their full potential.

Many of the girls have faced obstacles, limitations, fears, doubts, losses, and tests of their physical and mental endurance. They've all stumbled along the way but have refused to give up. Somehow, they knew their experiences—no matter how tough—would lead to something valuable. The pain, sweat, blood, and tears were worth it.

You may wonder where their daring comes from—and how you can challenge yourself. Or maybe you already have a courageous spirit and want to learn more about exciting adventures you might try. Either way, we hope this book encourages you to believe in your abilities, find activities that motivate and exhilarate you, test yourself, face hurdles with confidence, feel good about who you are and what you can do, and most of all, dream big.

Look around: Girls and young women who dare are every-where. They're the ones who try new things, go after their goals, take positive risks, stick up for themselves and their friends, and hold on to their beliefs despite the opinions of others. These young women are showing the world what they're made of . . . and you can, too.

If one of their adventures sparks your interest, you can check out the resources in the "Go Exploring" section at the end of the story. You'll find a variety of books, magazines, organizations, or Web sites that will tell you more about the activity you're interested in.

And if you want to learn about other women who have achieved remarkable things in their lives, take a look at the timelines on pages 238–252, which chronicle women's contributions in sports, travel, exploration, space, the Olympics, and the military. To find out more about any of these famous women, go to your local library for a biography or autobiography, or explore their history-making feats online.

After reading the stories in Part 1 of this book, you may feel like you're ready to start pursuing your own adventure. Part 2 tells you how to prepare yourself mentally and physically for the challenges that lie ahead. In "Getting Your Mind in Shape," you'll discover the importance of believing in yourself, having a positive attitude, setting goals, being confident, and more. In "Getting Your Body in Shape," you'll find out about the benefits of exercise and good nutrition, and how to make them both a part of your life. "Take Action" activities help you put all of these ideas to work.

Whether you stumble or fly, we're rooting for you. We believe that each step you take—forward or back—is an important part of your journey. No matter what happens, remember one thing: Just trying something new and doing your best is what makes you a true winner.

We hope that the remarkable accomplishments of the young women in this book inspire you to believe that you, too, can do anything!

If you want to write to us about this book, contact us care of:

Free Spirit Publishing Inc.
400 First Avenue North, Suite 616
Minneapolis, MN 55401-1724
help4kids@freespirit.com
http://www.freespirit.com

We look forward to hearing from you!

Tina Schwager and Michele Schuerger

PART 1:

Meet 25 Gutsy Girls

What does it take to climb a mountain, swim or sail the ocean, free-fall out of an airplane, travel to far-off places, brave below-zero temperatures, explore the remote wilderness, walk on a circus high wire, survive basic training at military school, become a world-class athlete, or accomplish the kind of daring feats most people only dream of? You're about to find out. In Part 1, twenty-five young women tell you what it's like to take life to the extreme.

Merrick Johnston
------------ Mountain Climber ------------

Birthdate: 1/18/83
Hometown: Anchorage, Alaska
School: Robert Service High School
Family: mom, Jennifer; dad, Allan;
brothers, Lauchlin (20) and Ross (19)
Hobbies: soccer, track, snowboarding,
tennis, skiing, wrestling

Because my entire state (Alaska) is one big playground, anytime I want an adventure, all I have to do is look in my own backyard. I've taken all of my friends on hikes, giving many of them their first true taste of Alaska. I think that many people who live here haven't learned to appreciate what this place has to offer; they seem to spend most of their time inside their houses or driving in their cars. If you get to know Alaska's terrain, life here can be extraordinary.

> "Getting to the top is no big deal; it's the journey along the way that matters."
>
> – Merrick

Hiking and spending time in the mountains are my favorite things to do. My mom runs her own company, Great Alaskan Gourmet Adventures, organizing adventures for people who want to explore the outdoors. I work with her as a guide. Together, we teach clients hiking and technical skills for rock and ice climbing, and we take them on all kinds of trips to places like Prospect Heights, Wolverine Peak, and Little Switzerland.

I've always loved hanging out with the mountaineers I've met through my mom's business. When I hear about their experiences, I think about the things I may be able to accomplish someday. Best of all, working as a guide has exposed me to the joy of mountain climbing at an early age.

When I was nine, I heard one of the more experienced climbers describe what it was like to scale Mount McKinley—the unpredictable climate; the challenging, icy terrain; the awesome feeling of reaching the summit. My interest was sparked right away.

Denali (Mt. McKinley's Indian name) is the highest peak in North America. At 20,320 feet, its arctic conditions make climbing Mt. McKinley a major test of personal strength, technical skill, and teamwork. I dreamed of climbing that icy peak . . . all I had to do was convince my mom I could!

Two years later, I finally won her over. My mom realized that I was serious about attempting "The High One," as Mt. McKinley is called. I was determined to become the youngest person to accomplish this feat (beating the boy who set the record before me).

I grew up with two older brothers, and most of my friends were boys. You might say I was just "one of the guys." I did everything they did, and more. By the time I was eight, I realized many girls were interested in different activities than boys. I also learned that the boys I hung out with thought they were naturally better athletes than the girls they knew. Well, this fired up my competitive spirit. I wanted to prove girls can do anything, and this helped fuel my desire to climb Mt. McKinley.

Although my mom had given in to my pleas to make the climb, she said I couldn't go on the expedition alone. We decided to attempt the ascent together, along with an experienced group of climbers. I knew I needed to be strong and fit to take on such a huge challenge.

I was already physically active, spending as much time as I could enjoying outdoor activities like skiing, snowboarding, canoeing, hiking, and rafting. I also played soccer, ran track, and did gymnastics. But it's not just fitness that counts when climbing: You must also have excellent mountaineering skills. On a mountain like Denali, I'd be facing life-threatening situations. If I didn't know what I was doing, I'd pose a threat to myself and to everyone else participating in the climb.

To help prepare for the expedition, my mom and I practiced our glacier-travel techniques, winter camping skills, and climbing with *crampons* (metal spikes clamped onto our boots). We also climbed Alaska's Mount Goode—a 10,900 foot peak in the Chugach Mountains—to test my high-altitude and cold-weather endurance. My mom trained with me daily on the Chugach Range, where I climbed with a 50 pound pack on my back. This helped build my strength and stamina, both of which are important for high-altitude climbing in cold conditions. Because the altitude can zap your strength, it's essential to develop deep reserves of energy to draw from.

We also became familiar with "crevasse rescue" (a crevasse is basically a deep crevice, often found in a glacier). Because glaciers are like large rivers that flow, ebb, and shift, deep crevasses form as the glaciers travel downward. The crevasses can be hundreds of feet deep, and if you fall in and are knocked unconscious, your climbing team must have the skills to haul you up safely with ropes.

Scaling mountains has always been a fun way for me to spend time. I enjoy the struggles and obstacles I face on the way up, and I like making decisions about the routes.

Mountain climbing gives me a whole differ-ent perspective on the world. When I'm on a mountain, I don't worry about any of the things that I worry about at home. I block out the rest of the world and just focus on the next step. I concentrate on my basic needs—having enough food and water,

Merrick *(right)* and her mom, Jennifer, take refuge in a snow cave while climbing Mt. McKinley.

how the weather will affect the climb, planning the next step, obstacles that may lie ahead. It's all about survival, self-reliance, and instinct.

My hiking and climbing experiences have taught me the importance of enjoying the moment. If your only concern is get-ting to the end of the hike or the top of the mountain, you miss out on all of the wonderful things that happen along the way. Whenever I reach the peak of a mountain, I make a point of enjoying the view and the beauty of my natural surroundings.

This means a lot more than just congratulating myself on getting to the top.

After I started preparing for the climb of my dreams, I discovered that my source of motivation had totally changed. Suddenly breaking a record no longer mattered to me. My new goal was simply to enjoy the climb. I also decided the climb shouldn't just be about me, so I collected pledges to raise money for a wellness and child-abuse-prevention center in Anchorage. The higher I climbed, the more money I'd raise for a good cause.

On June 1, 1995, we began our ascent to Denali's summit. Our group consisted of eight people, and we divided into two teams of four.

We carried enough food and fuel to weather any storms. Because hauling a lot of extra gear on our backs was difficult, we regularly loaded up sleds that held our extra food and fuel, then towed the sleds up about 1,000 feet, so we could bury the supplies. Then we returned to our starting point to spend the night.

The next day, if the weather was good, we'd climb to the place where our supplies were buried and begin the entire process again. (So, in a sense, we climbed the mountain twice!) This process took longer, but it gave our bodies a chance to become acclimated to the higher altitude, which meant a better night's sleep. Plus, if we were to get stuck on the mountain due to bad weather, we'd have enough supplies to last for a while.

I discovered that the worst thing to do while hiking up the mountain was to count my footsteps; once I started, it seemed I couldn't stop. Quite frequently on our ascent, I found myself counting my footsteps for hours. I'd try to occupy my mind by singing songs with my friend J.T., who hiked close to me. This helped me stop the endless counting, and I enjoyed the journey more.

As we made our way up the mountain, the weather was so bad that we had to stop for days at a time. Although it was June, the temperature hovered around 10 to 15 degrees during the day, and when the wind was blowing, the temperature dropped well below zero. Of the twenty-six days it took to complete the climb, we spent a total of thirteen unable to move.

How I got started:

A famous climber who visited my mom described the experience of climbing Mt. McKinley: This gave me the fever to climb it myself. Plus, I've always loved outdoor challenges.

Accomplishments:

I raised $3,800 for the Anchorage Center for Families, as a result of my climb. I'm a snowboarder, too—I won second overall in combined slalom and giant slalom in the 1997 National Snowboard Race (a slalom race is a course that tests precision, speed, and flexibility; the giant slalom is designed to test speed, strength, and tenacity). I recently qualified as a member of the USASA Junior National Snowboard Team.

How I stay motivated:

What motivates me is a desire to have fun, and I want to share this enthusiasm with other people. I give talks at schools to inspire other kids to take advantage of the natural world that surrounds them and not take for granted what's right outside their back door.

My future:

I love to stay busy while having fun. My goals are to go to Dartmouth College, go hang gliding off Mount Logan (in Canada's Yukon Territory), be the youngest person to climb Vinson Massif in Antarctica, go para-sailing with my snowboard, and enjoy my life.

We dug snow caves for shelter against dangerous blizzards. Inside the caves, we waited for the storms to end. At 17,200 feet, we had to stay in one spot for seven days in a row. We passed the time playing cards, reading, and singing songs.

We encountered some scary *whiteouts* on the trip. Whiteouts are usually caused by blizzards or extreme snowfall (sometimes by fog). When you're caught in a whiteout, you can't tell where the sky stops and the snow on the mountainside begins.

If I'm familiar with the area in which I'm climbing, whiteouts don't bother me (it's actually kind of fun to make a game out of looking for my friends). But one of the whiteouts we encountered on Denali was so intense that I could barely see my own feet.

When the whiteout hit, we were walking on a high ridge. The snow was coming down hard, and the temperature had plummeted to about 20 degrees below zero. I told myself to keep moving. I wasn't afraid, perhaps because I focused on walking instead of thinking about the danger I was in. Looking back, I remember the whiteout as a fun and exhilarating experience, although most of the team was scared.

The climb proved to be eventful in other ways, too. One day, we were on a ridge 3,000 feet above a crevasse. Everyone was in a bad mood because we were tired and cold (so cold that our eyelashes had frozen). Suddenly I lost my footing and slipped, falling toward the crevasse. As I slid, I reached out and by sheer luck, grabbed my mom's ax, which was stuck in the ice. I was extremely fortunate and fell only a short distance. Who knows how far I could have dropped!

As we approached 11,000 feet on our ascent, I had an even worse scare. Some of my gear was hanging on cords around my neck, including my lip balm, a Swiss army knife, and my sunscreen. The cords somehow got tangled up in the rope that was attached to my chest harness. Before I knew what was happening, the cords were strangling me. I started choking, and I tried to yell for help. The wind howled so loudly that no one could hear my cries.

I got scared and began hyperventilating, which frightened me more. Fortunately, the other team caught up to ours, saw what was happening, and helped me get untangled. It took a few minutes for me to calm down and breathe normally again, but I was ready to continue the climb.

Despite the obstacles we faced, including freezing weather and exhaustion, our group kept moving. Over and over, I told myself not to give up. On June 23—twenty-two days after we'd set out—we finally reached the peak.

What an amazing sight! We stood speechless, staring at the incredible view and the sunset that colored the clouds pink. I'll never forget how pure everything looked from Denali's summit. I huddled next to my mom, feeling awed and, most of all, proud. I had become the youngest person to climb Mt. McKinley, setting a new record.

Later, as we made our way down, I cried. Denali was so extraordinary, and I didn't want to leave it behind. For me, mountains are like a sanctuary, a place where I get to know myself. It's hard to explain how I feel in the mountains. All I know is I feel wonderful.

Go Exploring

Backpacking: A Woman's Guide by Adrienne Hall (Camden, ME: Ragged Mountain Press, 1998). Maybe you'll never climb a mountain, but you can have fun hiking and backpacking in the great outdoors. Written especially for women (teen girls can enjoy it, too), this book explains what you need to know to backpack: how to choose the right gear, plan a trip, carry your pack, prepare food, stay safe, and preserve the trails.

Epic: Stories of Survival from the World's Highest Peaks edited by Clint Willis (New York: Thunder's Mouth Press, 1997). Read fifteen true stories of heroic climbs (on mountains like Everest, K2, and the Himalayas) and the difficult situations the mountaineers faced.

Within Reach: My Everest Story by Mark Pfetzer and Jack Galvin (New York: EP Dutton, 1998). The youngest climber ever to attempt to ascend Mt. Everest, Mark Pfetzer recounts his experience on the mountain at age 18. The author shares his love of mountain climbing and his determination to pursue his dreams.

Christy Hauptman
-------------- Skydiver --------------

Birthdate: 3/3/81
Hometown: Maui, Hawaii
School: Seabury Hall
Family: mom, Patty; dad, Tom; stepmom,
Colleen; brothers, Cliff (18), Tommy (13),
and Joey (12); sisters, Amy (15),
Sasha (14), and Nikki (4)
Hobbies: dancing, acting, jet skiing, singing

M any people think of skydiving as the ultimate daredevil sport, but I don't see it that way. We all have something we like to do, and jumping out of planes just happens to be my "thing."

I don't ever want to look back on my life and think, "I should have done this or that" or "Why didn't I give it a try?" At some point, you have to make a leap of faith. It's in this moment— the leap—that you're really living. When you get over the fear of leaving the straight-and-narrow path and doing something out of the ordinary, you find out how exciting life can be.

"Facing your fears opens you up to all kinds of possibilities."

– Christy

My dad, who owns a helicopter business in Hawaii, started skydiving a few years ago. He and his friends let me tag along with them when they made their jumps. I had gone bungee jumping once before and loved the sensation. You'd think this would satisfy my desire to free fall, but all it did was make me crave an even bigger adrenaline rush!

Skydiving became the next thrill I wanted to experience, and I began to spend more time with my dad and his friends. I watched them jump from the plane, and I tried to learn from their techniques. For now, observing was the closest I could come to actually skydiving. Seeing everyone else jump made me want to do it even more.

In the summer of 1996, I got my first taste of what skydiving feels like. My dad took my siblings and me to the Flyaway simulator in Las Vegas, Nevada, to learn the basics of the sport. Instead of jumping out of a plane, we experienced skydiving in a wind tunnel (an indoor column of air 12 feet across and 21 feet high, with airspeeds up to 120 miles per hour). First, I took a short class that taught me all about body position and safety; then I put on a jumpsuit, strapped on a helmet, and gave "skydiving" a try.

Little did I know that when we returned to Maui, my dad had a major surprise planned. One morning, my stepmom, Colleen, asked me if I wanted to go with her to the hangar where my dad runs his business. On the way there, she started hinting that I might be able to skydive that day. I found out that my dad had set up my first *tandem* jump, which meant I'd be attached by a harness to an instructor, so we could jump together.

How I got started:

A friend of my dad's was really into bungee jumping, and one day, he and my dad took me up in a helicopter. I took the plunge, bungee jumping right out of the helicopter. I loved the sensation of free falling, and I decided that skydiving was the next thing I wanted to try.

Accomplishments:

So far, I've jumped out of an airplane more than 100 times. I'm very proud of each and every jump. I'm also proud of my volunteer work at a summer camp for kids with disabilities.

How I stay motivated:

Skydiving makes me feel like I'm on top of the world. I love the natural high that comes from skydiving, but the confidence it gives me means even more.

My future:

I live life with more exuberance than I used to, and I feel more inspired about everything from skydiving to schoolwork. My mind works overtime with so many ideas and plans for the future. Right now, I plan on going to college to earn a business degree, so I can start a business of my own one day. I'd also like to become an actress. If skydiving takes me down a different path, that's fine, too.

I was so excited when we arrived at the hangar. My dad and one of my brothers were there waiting for me. After I talked to the tandem instructor, she checked my body position and corrected it a bit. My enthusiasm was so high that I was practically jumping up and down. The instructor attached the harness and parachute (which feels like a heavy backpack) over the jumpsuit I was wearing.

Jumpsuits aren't required by the United States Parachute Association (USPA), but depending on the material and size, the suits can help skydivers control how fast they fall and give them more control over certain parts of their bodies. Tight jumpsuits made of a material like nylon allow for a quicker descent, for example, and looser-fitting jumpsuits help slow your fall. (Now that I'm more experienced, I typically wear just a pair of lightweight pants, like the kind you might wear when snowboarding, and a long-sleeved T-shirt.)

The instructor and I practiced our exit while the plane was still on the ground. I felt confident and assured about the jump. Soon it would be time for the real thing.

I don't think it had sunk in that I was *actually* going to jump . . . until we reached 12,000 feet. After I was hooked up to the instructor's harness, I got nervous. It seemed like a million thoughts were racing through my head, but I couldn't manage to say a word.

At 15,000 feet, the door of the plane flew open. A cold blast of air rushed in, blowing straight at my face. The noise was incredible: It reminded me of the sound of wind in your ears when riding a motorcycle. I was terrified!

I remember hearing someone shout, "Step out!" This is when the fear *really* set in.

My stomach dropped as I clamped my hands to the doorway with all my strength. I started cussing like crazy, and I couldn't stop yelling at my dad. I screamed, "There's no way I'm stepping out of this plane! I'll die if I do!" I've never been so scared in my entire life, and I've never sworn so much either, especially in my father's presence.

My dad tried to reassure me. "You'll be fine," he said. "This is what you *wanted* to do."

All of a sudden, my mind stopped whirling. I realized there was no turning back. The next thing I knew, I was out of the plane.

I can hardly describe the feeling of euphoria that came over me as I soared through the sky. I felt like a feather, totally weightless and free, as if nothing could touch me. The wind tingled on my skin, and even though I wasn't cold, I got the chills. It was the most unbelievable sensation I've ever experienced.

Time seemed to slow down while I was in the air. The free fall itself didn't last for more than a minute, but it felt much longer to me. After the colorful parachute was released, we flew under the canopy for several minutes. The whole time, all I could do was stare at everything around me. The drop zone was incredibly scenic: Everywhere I looked I saw mountains, greenery, houses, and miles and miles of ocean.

When we finally reached the ground, we landed feetfirst, then slid on our rear ends. At first, I was dazed, and I didn't know what to say or do. Then I just started babbling. I was so awed that I couldn't wait to jump again. Since then, I've had a lot of great jumps, but not one has ever felt like the first . . . none could.

For my sixteenth birthday, my dad took me to the Parachute Center in Lodi, California. It was spring break, and this trip gave me the opportunity to receive some formal skydiving instruction. I spent three days training and jumping, which allowed me to improve from "student" jumping status and earn my "A" rating license (the basic USPA license that signifies I've advanced beyond student level). My dad has been very supportive of my skydiving, and this bond we share has given us a lot of special time together.

Some of my friends still can't believe that I skydive; they say I'm crazy, but I know they're a little impressed. They have said, however, that I'm kind of intimidating because of the confidence I've gained from skydiving. This sport makes me feel like I can do anything. Ever since I started jumping, I don't let fear get in my way like I used to.

Now I'm able to look my problems in the face and tell myself that I can handle them. If something's really troubling me, I go skydiving, if possible. When I'm flying through the air, looking at the earth far below, everything seems smaller, including my problems. It's the best outlet I have—the best one I can imagine.

Of course, there are times when I think, "What if I die? What if my main parachute malfunctions . . . will I be able to pull the reserve (extra) parachute in time?" So far, I've been able to deal with these fears because I believe that life is about risk taking. When you're willing to take a leap, each day becomes more exciting and challenging. Risks give me something to wake up for in the morning.

Christy is ready to take the plunge over the island of Maui.

Unfortunately, I can't jump out of a plane anytime I feel like it because I have to plan ahead. When I'm stressed out but can't skydive, I write down my thoughts on paper, and this really helps me. Keeping a journal gives me a chance to sort through my feelings and see things more clearly.

I often write about the feelings of envy I get when I watch expert skydivers who jump with proficiency and ease. Because I want to be as good as they are, I try to imitate their style, but usually I can't do as well. They have much more experience than I do. It helps to tell myself that, at one point, the experts were where I am now. I know that if I keep practicing, my jumps will improve.

I want to do something great with my life, and I see skydiving as good preparation for future challenges. It's taught me to be brave, confident, and most of all, to have faith in myself. I've looked death in the face on about 113 occasions, and I've survived. That's pretty cool.

Go Exploring

Parachuting: The Skydiver's Handbook by Dan Poynter and Mike Turoff (Santa Barbara, CA: Para Publishing, 1998). This informative reference guide has photos and drawings for thrill-seekers interested in skydiving. You'll find basic to advanced techniques, emergency procedures, and a list of skydiving centers.

Parachute Center
12597 N. Highway 99
Acampo, CA 95220
(209) 369-1128
http://www.parachutecenter.com

The Parachute Center's state-of-the-art equipment and USPA-certified instructors can help improve your skydiving skills, no matter what your level of experience. You must be 18 years of age to begin skydiving. Their Web site includes a photo album, log book, and links to other skydiving sites.

Carmella House

---- U.S. Naval Academy Midshipman ----

Birthdate: 11/3/78
Hometown: Fort Branch, Indiana
School: U.S. Naval Academy
Family: mom, Mariette; dad, Donald;
sister, Analda (23)
Hobbies: flying, piano, chess,
debate team, pistol team, travel, tennis

My main passion in life is flying; it pervades my every thought. I find it exhilarating, like I'm dancing among the clouds, totally in control of my fate.

Somehow I always knew I'd get my private pilot's license as soon as I was old enough. But when I actually flew solo for the first time at sixteen and made my first flight as a licensed pilot at seventeen, it seemed hard to believe. As a little girl, I imagined flying planes, piloting jets, and eventually becoming an astronaut. This has always been my dream, and now I'm on the path to making it come true.

To reach my goal, I planned to attend the U.S. Naval Academy in Annapolis, Maryland, and pursue an advanced degree in astrophysics. I was accepted to the Academy, and my first challenge was to survive six rigorous weeks of basic training before school officially began in the fall. July 1, 1997, marked Induction Day, or "I-Day," for the Class of 2001.

New midshipmen (students of the Academy) are known as "plebes," which is why basic training is referred to as "Plebe Summer." All of the plebes, including me, reported to the Academy at 7 A.M. on I-Day, and we spent the next several hours waiting in line—for haircuts, blood tests, and our uniforms and gear.

In the late afternoon, we went to the Induction ceremony. Here all of the newcomers to the Academy were required to take the Oath of Office of a Midshipman—pledging to do our jobs to the best of our abilities and to uphold the values of honor, courage, and commitment.

I took the oath with all of the other plebes, then spent time visiting with my parents. Following the ceremony, we all said good-bye to our families, then headed back to Bancroft Hall, our dormitory.

Plebe Summer had officially begun.

Plebes have virtually no rights, privileges, personalities, individuality, or respect. What plebes *do* have is a ton of rules and responsibilities. Plebes can't speak unless spoken to, and when responding, can use only five basic responses:

"Sir, yes, sir."
"Sir, no, sir."
"Sir, no excuse, sir."
"Sir, I'll find out, sir."
"Sir, aye, aye, sir."

(Sir is replaced with ma'am when appropriate.)

All of this has a purpose: As a plebe, you start at the lowest level and are trained to learn, respond quickly, obey orders, respect authority, perform, and ultimately, to make good leadership decisions under pressure.

All of the plebes became part of a *company,* or unit, consisting of anywhere between 130 and 150 members (there was a total of thirty companies). Each company was further divided into four *platoons.* And the platoons were made up of three *squads* of about 10–12 people. Our *squad leaders* had the authority to tell us what to do.

> "The only limits you really face are those you put on yourself."
> – Carmella

Each day, we read material from a pocket-sized book called *Reef Points,* which was like a bible to us. It contained everything from naval history, to information about the Academy, to military song lyrics, to facts about ships and aircraft. We were required to know this book inside and out because at any moment we might be verbally tested on it.

At 5:15 A.M., *reveille* (a bugle call) signaled the beginning of the day. As plebes, we were required to gather in the hallway "braced up" (eyes forward, back against the wall, chin tucked deep into the chest), dressed in gym gear, and holding the sheets from our "racks," or bunk beds. We had to drink a full cup of water for hydration, and then we were given one or two minutes

How I got started:

My sister sparked my interest in the space program when she attended Space Camp at the U.S. Space and Rocket Center in Huntsville, Alabama, in 1987. I went to Space Camp for the first time when I was in fifth grade, and by the spring of my senior year in high school, I had returned 19 times to attend different sessions.

Accomplishments:

1998: First place and Navy Commendation in the First Annual Ethics Essay Competition; first place, Tri-Service Military Academy Powerlifting Championships (198 pound class). 1997: National Merit finalist; Outstanding Junior Scientist of the Year at Indiana Junior Academy of Science (IJAS); Academic All-State in swimming. 1996: Right Stuff Award in Aviation Challenge (U.S. Space Academy); first-place winner in the senior division in science and math, and overall grand award winner (senior division) at the Hoosier State Science and Engineering Fair; first place and grand award winner in physics at the 47th International Science and Engineering Fair.

How I stay motivated:

Part of my motivation is that I want to fly high-performance jet aircraft and work in space for the thrill of the adventure. But I'm also greatly motivated by the desire to help other people. It fills me with great pride knowing that I'm serving my country. I have a deep respect and appreciation for this country, and I would give my life in her defense.

My future:

Right now, I'm majoring in physics, and by overloading my schedule and keeping my grades high, I hope to qualify for the Academy's Voluntary Graduate Education Program, which allows first-class midshipmen to begin graduate work during senior year. My ultimate goal is to become an astronaut and travel in space as a mission specialist, conducting experiments on space walks or aboard a space shuttle. One day, I'd like to return to the Academy to teach.

to make our beds. After the allotted time, the racks were inspected, and because we never passed inspection, the drill began all over again and continued for about a half hour.

Then we ran out to Turf Field for PEP (Plebe Exercise Program) at 6 A.M. This involved a series of calisthenics and sprints, usually followed by a platoon run. PEP lasted for about an hour, followed by morning quarters formation (the first military drill of the day) and breakfast at 7:45.

During meals, each squad sat at a table with their squad leader. The upperclassmen were served before the plebes. We constantly had to ask if the upperclassmen wanted more food or drink refills. We ate looking straight ahead and had to place our hands in our laps, under the table, after each bite or sip. While we ate, our squad leader asked us questions based on *Reef Points,* and if we didn't know the answer, we had to report back with the correct response before the next meal.

Everyone spoke to us in a shout. We were led from each day's training session by our squad leaders, speed-walking in single file, eyes forward, no speaking allowed. We could never just walk through the halls, we had to "chop." Chopping means running down the center of the "decks," or hallways, with high knees, looking straight ahead, squaring all corners, greeting any upperclassmen who walk by, and sounding off with "Go Navy, sir!" or "Beat Army, sir!"

As plebes, we were always sweaty, smelly, running late, and messing up. We never got anything right as plebes.

At the end of the day, we had about twenty minutes of personal time, which was barely enough time to take a shower, read the required materials, and write our "Thought of the Day" for the squad leader. The Thought of the Day served as a way for plebes to vent frustrations or bring up issues. Squad leaders used these writings to monitor our progress and spot any potential problems. (After Plebe Summer ended, the Thoughts of the Day were returned to each plebe, as a record of all we'd been through.)

At 9:40 P.M., each company gathered in their respective hallways for "Blue and Gold," which was the time for upperclassmen to make announcements and to comment on the plebes' performance. Although Blue and Gold was supposed to be the motivational high point of the day, ending with everyone singing "Navy Blue and Gold," it was usually a negative experience. Positive comments about our performance were few and far between.

"Lights Out" occurred at 10:00 each night. Everyone had to be in bed, under the sheets, and quiet. In my platoon, our commander would walk through the halls right after Lights Out yelling, "Congratulations, second platoon. Today you completed training day number (whatever it was). Tomorrow is a new day! Ooo-rah!" Then we'd yell and scream and beat on the walls, all in the name of motivation. This was actually the best part of the day! Not only were we finally able to get some rest, but we were reminded of everything we'd accomplished. Plus, we could smile in the dark and no one would know (since plebes were only allowed to smile or laugh while off duty).

When I was accepted to the Academy, my biggest fear was surviving Plebe Summer. Although the goal of basic training is to make plebes stronger and more disciplined, the techniques for arriving at this goal seem senseless and punishing. I realized that these techniques were grounded in tradition, but I wasn't sure if I'd have the strength to handle the pressure.

Toward the end of the first week of basic training, I began to question my decision to study at the Academy. One of my main problems was that I wasn't a good runner. During every run, I had a hard time keeping up with the others. I told myself that I could do it if I just put my mind to it, but a stronger voice inside me kept shouting, "Just take the easy way out!" Then one of my roommates left, adding to my uncertainty. Once she was gone, quitting seemed like a tempting option.

Of course, deep down, I didn't really want to leave. I was following my dream, and giving up would have been the end of my world as I knew it. I was torn: Part of me wanted to talk myself into giving up, but the other, stronger part of me just couldn't. I realized that I loved almost everything about the Academy, the Navy, and the military, and I was determined to make it. Those few days of doubt rejuvenated my dream.

Now, when I look back, I sometimes feel ashamed that I ever thought of leaving the Academy. Then again, I know that self-doubt plagues everyone at some point in their lives. When you have reservations, it may be a sign that you need to stop and reexamine your priorities. What do you really want to do? What's stopping you? How can you press on despite obstacles? I know now, without a doubt, that I made the right choice to stay at the Academy.

Getting through each day of Plebe Summer was a big accomplishment, but I thrived on the challenge. During the toughest days, my roommates and company-mates reminded me that I could do it, and they encouraged me not to give up. With their help, I focused on where all of my hard work would lead me in the future.

Carmella sits at the controls of a Cessna 172.

At the end of the six weeks of basic training, I was extremely proud to have faced the first (and one of the toughest) challenges of the Naval Academy. The experience taught me a lot about myself and what I'm able to handle. Perhaps the biggest lesson I learned is that mental determination and positive thinking are the keys to success.

Parents' Weekend followed, and my family had planned to visit me. All of the plebes were dressed in summer whites, and we marched over to the parade field where we were dismissed one company at a time. Alpha Company, the one I was in, got dismissed first, and we all just stood there for a second trying to figure out what to do.

Then we noticed the area where we were supposed to meet our families. At first, I couldn't find my parents, but suddenly I heard my mother's voice behind me calling out, "There she is!" I turned around, and she was running toward me with out-stretched arms. I didn't want to cry and managed to make it through her hug with dry eyes, but I couldn't stop the tears when I hugged my dad. My dad is a quiet man, and as we embraced, I remembered the encouraging letter he had written to me after the first week of Plebe Summer, when I was doubting my ability to persevere.

Both of my parents were so proud of me. I was excited to have my first "liberty" (free time), but I was also thoroughly exhausted, both mentally and physically. I couldn't believe that Plebe Summer was behind me. Now I was a full-fledged member of the U.S. Naval Academy. I'd actually made it!

Go Exploring

For more information about the Academy, contact the United States Naval Academy, Dean of Admissions, 117 Decatur Road, Annapolis, MD 21402-5017. Or visit the Academy online at: *http://www.nadn.navy.mil.*

Amelia Earhart's Daughters: The Wild and Glorious Story of American Women Aviators from World War II to the Dawn of the Space Age by Leslie Haynsworth and David M. Toomey (New York: William Morrow & Co., 1998). This book details the dramatic history of female aviators who challenged stereotypes and broke barriers in the early twentieth century, paving the way for today's women to pursue their love of sky and space.

U.S. Astronaut Hall of Fame
6225 Vectorspace Boulevard
Titusville, FL 32780
(407) 269-6100
http://www.astronauts.org

Log onto this Web site to get a virtual tour of the U.S. Astronaut Hall of Fame, home to the largest collection of astronaut artifacts. You can also get the latest news from the "out of this world" world of space exploration and hook up with other space-related links. Or write or call the Hall of Fame to get the information you're looking for.

U.S. Space Camp/Aviation Challenge
P.O. Box 070015
Huntsville, AL 35807-7015
1-800-63SPACE (1-800-637-7223)
http://www.spacecamp.com

Find out what it's like to be an astronaut (in Space Camp and Space Academy) or experience fighter-pilot training (in Aviation Challenge). The programs, which are divided into different age levels, include basic classroom learning and hands-on experience. The Web site is your online resource for everything you want to know about each program, including what you'll do there, rates, and the latest Space Camp news.

Nahara Rodriguez

Birthdate: 6/16/83
Hometown: Philadelphia, Pennsylvania
School: Widener Memorial
Family: mom, Diana; dad, Wilfredo; brothers,
Willie (25), Jonathan (21), Michael (20),
José (18), and Daniel (16)
Hobbies: singing, drawing, computer
animation, reading, swimming

On February 5, 1998, I was sitting in the grand ballroom of Philadelphia's St. Joseph's University, filled with pride. Hundreds of other people sat in the room, but I hardly noticed. I was too overcome by my emotions.

Surrounded by those who meant more to me than anyone in the world (my mom and dad, my grandmother, one of my brothers, and my coach), I was about to be honored for doing something I've always loved—swimming. I couldn't believe what was happening . . . *me,* the 1998 recipient of the Wilma Rudolph Courage Award.

The Philadelphia chapter of the Women's Sports Foundation presents the Courage Award (in honor of Wilma Rudolph) to a female athlete who has put forth a courageous effort or made a big comeback. To be honest, when I found out that I had won the award, I didn't know who Wilma Rudolph was. I went straight to the library and looked up her name in an encyclopedia. After reading her biography, I was really amazed. I never would have thought that I had something in common with such an incredible athlete.

Wilma Rudolph, an African-American athlete, suffered from polio as a child, and she wore a leg brace on her left leg until she was nine—but this didn't stop her from becoming an Olympian. She won a bronze medal in the 400 meter relay at the 1956 Olympic Games, and she received three gold medals at the 1960 Olympics in the 100, 200, and 400 meter relays. She was the first American woman to win three gold medals in track.

"Life is like a ladder. You may take one step up and then two down, but you just have to keep going until you reach the top."

— Nahara

An inspiration to athletes and other people worldwide, Wilma Rudolph created a foundation to help underprivileged children get involved in sports. She believed that athletics could help young people feel good about themselves and learn to pursue their dreams.

I could hardly believe after all I'd been through, after all that had happened to me, that I was actually winning this award. As I listened to my personal story being told to the audience, I thought back to the events that had led to this moment.

I was asleep in the back of my family's van when lights woke me. We were returning home late at night, from a restaurant at the beach near my home in Mayagüez, Puerto Rico, after celebrating a big contract my uncle had just signed. It was June 25, 1992.

I opened my eyes in time to see the bright headlights of an oncoming car. I grabbed my six-year-old cousin, who was sleeping next to me, and held her in my arms. I felt the impact, a crunch of metal. The van spun around, and everything became a blur.

I recall seeing myself on the floor of the van, while paramedics tried to help me. (Somehow, I was having an out-of-body experience. It felt like a dream.) I woke up in the hospital and asked the nurses what happened. They told me I'd been in an accident but the paramedics had done their best to fix me up. I also learned that my cousin was okay.

A drunk driver had run a red light, which caused the crash. He was twenty-one and had no driver's license; the car he was driving didn't even belong to him. After hitting us, he ran away from the scene but later came back with the police.

One drunk driver changed my destiny in a matter of seconds. I was severely injured, paralyzed from the waist down. Yet, he received only one month in jail and five months' probation as punishment.

For two weeks, I stayed in intensive care, with internal bleeding, collapsed lungs that had filled with blood, a broken back, and damage to my spinal cord. The doctors in Puerto Rico pretty much gave up on me. They kept telling my family and me that I'd never walk again or even be able to sit up by myself.

It was discouraging for me to hear the doctors predict all of the things I'd never do again. They didn't talk about things I might eventually be *able* to do. My mom was angered by their prognosis, and she wasn't willing to accept that there was no hope for me.

A friend of our family told my mom about the miraculous things that Shriners Hospital in Philadelphia, Pennsylvania, was

How I got started:

My dad taught me to swim when I was four years old and how to scuba dive when I was eight. I remember the oxygen tanks being so heavy that I'd practically topple over! But the tanks felt much lighter in the ocean, and under the water's surface, I glided with ease.

Accomplishments:

I play wheelchair hockey, tennis, and newcomb (a game similar to volleyball). Also, I was one of the top ten finalists in the 1998 Miss Pennsylvania American Junior Teen Pageant, where I won "Miss Personality."

How I stay motivated:

What keeps me going is my belief in God and the hope I have for tomorrow . . . that things will be better not only for me but also for those who are worse off than I am. I also receive comfort and encouragement from my parents and family. Most of all, I'm motivated by my goal to succeed in the future.

My future:

My dream is to someday be a singer, model, or computer animation specialist. I really don't know what God has planned for me in the future, but as long as I have my family, friends, and everyone I care about with me, anything can happen.

doing for people with spinal cord injuries. My mother called the hospital to discuss my situation, and the doctors there agreed to take me on as a patient. Because Shriners helps families in need, we wouldn't have to worry about medical insurance or paying our hospital bills. The hospital promised to take complete care of me.

There was just one catch—we had to arrange our own transportation to the United States.

I was in critical condition, so the commercial airlines we contacted refused to transport me. The airlines weren't equipped to accommodate a passenger who had to travel lying down.

Our only option was to hire a private air ambulance, as well as a doctor and nurse, to transport us to the United States. At $11,000, the cost was a big problem. My parents asked relatives for help, held raffles to raise money, and spoke with a TV reporter in Puerto Rico. He talked about me on TV, and soon signs were posted all over the city asking for donations. My family also sold many of our belongings for money. A week later, we were on our way to Philadelphia.

I was scared to leave my country. I wondered what America would be like and if the people there would be friendly. I knew that I would receive better medical care in the United States, but I felt sad leaving behind family and friends in Puerto Rico. It was a difficult, but hopeful, time for me.

Another thing that scared me was not knowing English. I was afraid that I wouldn't be able to communicate with the doctors and nurses in the United States. The only person in my family who spoke any English was my mother (and she spoke very little of it). We ended up having to get an interpreter.

I was in bad shape when I got to Shriners. Because of the poor medical care I had received in Puerto Rico, blood clots had formed in my legs. The first thing the doctors did was perform laser surgery to remove them.

After I was stabilized, I had my second surgery. This time, the doctors operated on my back. They placed metal rods in my spine, so I could sit up. A month later, I started physical therapy. The only way I could get around was in a wheelchair.

After I started physical therapy, I realized that what I really wanted was to swim again. I've always loved being in the water. Back home in Puerto Rico, my family spent a lot of time at the beach. When I swam, I felt like I could fly. Now that I couldn't walk, I was eager to be in the water. More than anything, I wanted to get out of my wheelchair and experience the freedom and weightlessness of swimming.

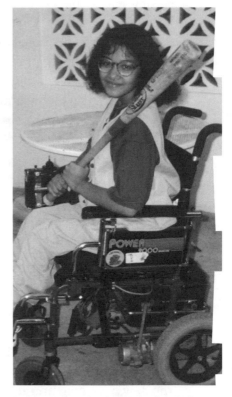

Eight weeks after the metal rods were placed in my back, I got into a pool for the first time since the accident. Swimming felt so liberating—like I was totally and completely free.

I thought that our stay in America would be temporary. I was wrong. The doctors decided I needed

Nahara stays active by playing baseball.

long-term medical care. If I wanted to get the best medical treatment, my family would have to make a home in Philadelphia, instead of returning to Puerto Rico.

My story appeared on the Philadelphia TV news, and a Puerto Rican woman who was watching (I now call her "Aunt Juanita") decided to help out my family. Although she didn't know us and didn't have much money, Aunt Juanita took the time to get us situated in the city. A friend of hers, Olga Detres, helped out, too. Both of them made sure we had breakfast, dinner, clothing, and a place to sleep. With their assistance, my family found an apartment, my dad got a job at a furniture store, and two of my brothers joined us from Puerto Rico. All of us are so grateful for the kindness of Aunt Juanita and Olga.

I had to stay in the hospital for almost a year. After I went home, I continued outpatient physical therapy for two more years.

As part of my therapy, the doctors put electrodes into my leg muscles to help them contract (I wasn't able to contract them on my own). Because I had no feeling in my legs, I didn't need anesthesia for the surgery. I was awake the whole time, watching a videotape of the movie *Pinocchio*.

The electrodes helped with my therapy; I got to the point where I could stand up, which was a major accomplishment. Things were looking good until my body started to reject the electrodes. They had to be removed to avoid infection.

Swimming, my favorite activity in the world, helped me to stay strong and positive. My swim coach, Mr. Schanlon (the one who nominated me for the Wilma Rudolph Courage Award), worked with me in the pool and let me teach class sometimes. Being in the water made me feel like I was in a different world.

Over time, I learned that the best therapy for me was athletics. In addition to swimming, I got involved in wheelchair hockey, baseball, and tennis, and did exercises several times a week on my own at home or in gym class at school. I even started taking scuba-diving lessons.

In the future, I hope to start diving again. Because of the damage to my lungs from the accident, I have to be cautious when I dive in the ocean. I can only go down 10 to 15 feet, or I start to hyperventilate. But, to me, it doesn't matter how deep I go—I'm just excited to do whatever I can.

These days, I don't get to swim as much as I'd like to because I'm so busy with schoolwork and extracurricular activities. But sometimes my dad takes me to the river, where I swim and play for hours. Whenever I'm worried, mad, or upset, swimming releases the pressure and helps me relax. Being in the water is like emotional therapy for me.

I never imagined that swimming would take me to such amazing places in my life. In January 1998, when my coach told me that he'd nominated me for an award for my swimming, I thought it was a really nice thing to do. But then the whole thing slipped my mind. A week later, he came up to me all excited and said, "You won! You won!" I was surprised.

I thought that I might receive a trophy and be told that I'd done a good job with my swimming. But when my mom was asked to sign release forms, allowing my picture to appear in the newspaper, it started to sink in that winning this award was a much bigger deal than I had originally thought. I figured that I'd better find out who Wilma Rudolph was and why I deserved to be honored in her name.

When the audience at the award ceremony gave me a standing ovation, I started to cry, and so did my mom. I'd never had so many people stand up for me and applaud. I was proud and excited, and I felt like all my hard work had been worth it.

The certificate I won hangs in a frame in our living room. When I look at my award, it reminds me that things do turn out okay. Other people in this world have suffered more than I have, and when I compare myself to them, I realize that I don't have it so bad.

Recently, I was in the hospital for a kidney infection. My roommate there had become paralyzed from a car accident on her eighteenth birthday. She was really depressed, and I started talking to her about my own experience and about having faith that things will work out. I told her that, no matter what, she shouldn't give up.

After my accident and throughout my recovery, I gained courage from my parents and from my faith in God. I came to believe that whatever happens in life has a purpose and that

God has a reason for everything . . . even for me being paralyzed. The day I talked to my roommate at the hospital, my courage and faith were renewed.

No matter how tough things get in life, don't ever give up. That's what I tell others, and it's what I tell myself.

Go Exploring

Wilma Rudolph by Tom Biracree (Broomall, PA: Chelsea House Publishing, 1991). This book tells Wilma Rudolph's courageous story of overcoming polio to rise to Olympic greatness.

National Sports Center for the Disabled
P.O. Box 1290
Winter Park, CO 80482
(303) 316-1540
http://www.nscd.org/nscd/

"No mountain too high" is this organization's motto. The center offers year-round recreational and competitive challenges, including skiing, snow-boarding, biking, hiking, in-line skating, sailing, and whitewater rafting.

Wheelchair Sports, U.S.A.
3595 E. Fountain Boulevard, Suite L-1
Colorado Springs, CO 80910
(719) 574-1150
http://www.wsusa.org

Recreational and competitive programs for all age groups are available through Wheelchair Sports, U.S.A. Regional organizations offer activities like swimming, track, and basketball.

Meredith Mendelson

Ocean Sailor

Birthdate: 12/17/78
Hometown: Pittsburgh, Pennsylvania
School: Bates College
Family: mom, Sherry; dad, Gib
Hobbies: sailing team, college radio
disc jockey, knitting, writing

T he ocean is an amazing, powerful, and overwhelming presence. It can force you to examine yourself and your surroundings in ways you might never have considered before. While at sea, I felt as if I developed an intimacy with the ocean. I believe that you have to experience the ocean, and know it personally, before you can fully respect its strength and beauty. What I learned at sea continues to influence my life on land. I know that the ocean will always be a part of me.

My semester at sea began in St. Thomas, in the U.S. Virgin Islands, February 3, 1997 (the year before I left for college). I was participating in Ocean Classroom, a program for high school students interested in learning about life at sea. The moment I was dockside, the crew put me to work, and the work didn't end until I met my family in Boston seventeen weeks later.

From the start, there was a month's worth of provisions to store belowdecks, the names of lines and sails to learn, and bunks to arrange. Obviously, this wasn't going to be a pleasure trip on a cruise ship, but I already knew that! We were aboard a 131 foot gaff-rigged schooner called the *Harvey Gamage.* (This type of ship carried commerce around the world in the late nineteenth century. The schooner was authentic in its construction but appointed with modern equipment.)

The captain of the schooner that would serve as our new home introduced himself and the crew. He told us that on our journey there would be times when we'd be exhausted, exhilarated, angry, overwhelmed, and frustrated—but all the while, we'd be having the time of our lives.

The ship looked so beautiful as we readied her for the trip to sea. Our journey would take us from St. Thomas to St. John, Dominica, St. Lucia, Grenada, the Grenadines, Guadeloupe, Antigua, Puerto Rico, the Dominican Republic, Haiti, and the Bahamas. Then we'd head to Cumberland Island (on the Georgia coast); Beaufort, North Carolina; St. Michaels, Maryland; New

York City; and Mystic, Connecticut. Lastly, we'd go from Gloucester, Massachusetts, to Boston. Once we set sail, we wouldn't be near land for days on end.

The anchor was raised, and a crowd milled around the foredeck. In the distance, islands cast uneven shadows against the horizon as the sun set behind them. It was the start of an amazing journey, where each new day promised difficult, but welcome, challenges.

I wondered what kind of person I'd be when I returned home in June. Would I be different? Would I feel comfortable among my friends? How would I seem on the outside? Inside, would I be constantly attuned to boat schedules and weather patterns? I felt an over-load of new sensations and emotions—too many to untangle just then.

> "I've come to realize that all passages are a way of knowing—and a way of recognizing what we *don't* know."
>
> – Meredith

There were sixteen students aboard, ranging in grade level from freshmen to seniors, plus two teachers, a tutor (the captain's wife), six professional crew members, the cook, and of course, the captain. Every member of the crew was an invaluable resource for me, and I consider several of them to be the greatest mentors of my life. We studied, among other subjects, maritime literature and history, marine biology, applied maritime mathematics (primarily how sails make a ship move), and navigation.

For me, the biggest challenge was adjusting to the routine of life on a ship. I shared a tiny cabin with another girl, and I had a difficult time dealing with the lack of space. Whenever all of us went ashore, we did so in small groups—never alone.

As an only child, I'd grown accustomed to having time alone and plenty of personal space. On the schooner, I had neither. Personal needs weren't a priority; there were bigger concerns. One of the main objectives of the program was to instill a strong group mentality, in which individuals came to count on each other to reach common goals.

On a schooner, there's nowhere to hide. If you're scared or insecure, you can't run away from these feelings or hide them from other people: You have to face them or share them. As a group, we learned to rely on each other for support.

Meredith does one of her chores aboard the *Harvey Gamage.*

The atmosphere on board the ship was often tense (this can happen in any small, isolated community). We were a group of independent people with varied personalities trying to work together in close quarters. Although we aimed for teamwork and harmony, sometimes tempers flared and the tension became thick.

When problems arose, the captain's word was law; no one was allowed to question his commands. This hierarchical concept was new to me—I had grown up in a family that carefully weighed my opinions. I came to realize that life aboard a ship is very different from life on land. At sea, there isn't always time to consider options, think through things carefully, or reach a compromise. Some decisions have to be made in a split second.

Whether at sea or at port, our work on the schooner was never done. One of the duties was *tarring* (rubbing oil on) the *stays* (steel cables that support the ship's mast, which in turn supports the sails). The sails were harder to raise if the stays hadn't been tarred recently, so one of my tasks was to be hoisted high up along the stays in the *boatswain's chair* (a swing-like seat you sit on when being raised in the air) to rub oil into the steel-cable stays with a rag. It was a thankless task. No one ever noticed if the stays were tarred until they needed to be tarred again.

By the end of each day, we fell into our bunks like dead weight. Our duties were physically and emotionally taxing, and we had to do everything exactly as we were told.

Someone had to be on watch twenty-four hours a day, seven days a week. Each watch rotation lasted four hours, with four or five students on each shift (under the observation of a mate and a deckhand). On bow lookout, we kept a constant watch on the water for other ships; we were taught to recognize the size, type, and direction of other vessels by reading their navigation lights. We also kept a lookout for buoys, reefs, whales, and dolphins. Anything we saw was reported to the watch officer.

Standing at the forward end of the ship, peering at the wide expanse of sea, could be overwhelming. The experience made me feel small and insignificant, perhaps even inconsequential. I came to regard bow lookout as the lookout of humility and wonder.

- - - - - - - -

Life at sea, particularly on a majestic, tall wooden ship, is about tradition. When I finally allowed myself to accept this way of life, I became more aware of the importance of my individual actions and began to take pride in any menial task. Although I was never singled out for a job well done, I came to realize that recognition isn't as important as personal satisfaction and achievement.

Once I got past my exhaustion and allowed myself to be humbled, the magnitude of the whole experience at sea overtook me. A month into our adventure, we were sailing near the Virgin Islands. The clouds made shadowy patches on the sky's periwinkle coat; on the edges of the horizon were hues of emerald and purple. I heard a radio operator call a boat out at sea.

As I heard the call, I thought about how alone we were on the ship. No one knew our exact location, but our radio contact on land could track us down if necessary. For the moment, though, we were out of sight of everything but the sea. In a way, I felt both lost and located at the same time.

Night fell. Above me, the mainsail in its *wing-on-wing* position (which maximizes the sail area receiving wind) loomed reassuringly. The water below was as dark and shiny as an oil slick. A scattering of dotted lights in the distance illuminated the streets and houses of an island. With the wind whipping against my face and the beautiful images surrounding me, I didn't want morning to come.

Life on a ship, especially at night, brings you more in tune with yourself. Darkness heightens your senses, making you more aware of sounds and smells. I could almost hear my heartbeat as we cut through the water, forging a passage through time and space.

The mainsail pushed forward as the wind caught it. Soon the whole world brightened, and the sky turned a peach-tea color. I was there to greet the new day.

Days in port were as busy as our days at sea. We were on deck at 7:15 A.M. and had the ship, both above and belowdecks, cleaned by eight. This meant scrubbing the decks, polishing the brass, and cleaning the "head" (bathroom).

We shared galley rotation, or kitchen duty. The galley "slave" had to help cook, wash dishes, and clean up after the meal. After breakfast, we were usually ashore by 9:30, ready to explore the nearby island or town on foot (occasionally by van) and perhaps visit a market or museum.

I enjoyed meeting and talking to the island residents and the locals in eastern seaboard towns. Visiting places like Haiti and other tiny islands in the Caribbean opened my eyes to lifestyles that differ greatly from my own. More often than not, I realized how much I had in common with the people I met. The people were friendly, generous, and eager to share their world and learn about ours. Oceans may separate landmasses, but as a sailor, I came to see that oceans are our links to one another.

This voyage left me with many lasting impressions, but I carry in my heart one memory that, for me, embodies the whole experience. This defining moment occurred on our last full day at sea, heading to Gloucester over Stellwagon Bank, a shallow area of Cape Cod Bay.

How I got started:

I applied to Ocean Classroom (my semester at sea) after receiving literature about the program from my headmistress during my junior year. She knew of my interest in sailing and that I was planning to graduate a year early to study in a less traditional way before heading to college.

Accomplishments:

Aside from my achievements related to Ocean Classroom (including editing the ship newsletter), I edited my high school literary magazine and won creative-writing prizes my junior and senior years. As a college freshman, I was awarded the first-year writing prize.

How I stay motivated:

I do my best work under pressure. The ship was always a busy place; I had a lot to do and not much time to do it in. This really kept me on my toes.

My future:

I plan to be an environmental studies major with a focus on fisheries management and marine policy. I also intend to spend a semester at the Williams-Mystic program at Mystic Seaport Museum during my junior year of college (this program combines academics and the study of oceans).

It was around 9 A.M., and I had just come off sunrise watch. One of the other students spotted a humpback whale *breaching* (leaping out of the water) off the starboard bow. This marked the first time we'd seen humpbacks during the entire trip.

To get a better view, we all rushed up onto the *mastheads* (tops of the masts), which the captain and mates normally wouldn't allow. We watched in awe as the pod of whales circled us, silent as shadows. We stayed aloft for what seemed like hours, unified by the amazing spectacle of tail fins and breaches.

Suddenly the silence was shattered by a cavalcade of whale-watching boats coming east from Gloucester. Tourists hung on the railings of the boats, "oohing" and "aahing" as they pointed at the whales. The noise disturbed the peaceful scene, and the whales slowly swam away. The intimacy of our encounter with these incredible creatures was broken.

In that moment, the teachings of the journey—respect for the mystery of the sea and appreciation for the ancient traditions of maritime science—became crystal clear to me. The very things that threaten fragile marine ecosystems (such as motor-boats and diesel fuels) confronted us in the form of a whale-watching boat.

I looked at the expressions on the faces of my fellow ship-mates, and I knew they were feeling what I was feeling: anger, frustration, pride, sadness. I knew, in that moment, our perception of the ocean and our place in the world had been forever altered.

If you are willing to be humbled, go to sea. Let the ocean overtake you. Don't fight the lessons it can teach.

Go Exploring

Maiden Voyage by Tania Aebi (New York: Ballantine Books, 1989). This is the story of the first American woman, and the youngest person ever, to circumnavigate the globe solo. Tania tells of her two-and-a-half-year journey, both spiritual and personal, which began when her father gave her the choice of a college education or a 26 foot sloop . . . but if she picked the boat, she had to sail it around the world—alone.

Schooner Harvey Gamage Foundation, Inc.
P.O. Box 446
Cornwall, NY 12518
1-800-724-7245
http://www.sailgamage.org

Find out about the Foundation's learning, adventure, and discovery programs, which vary in length (from one week to an entire semester). They include Ocean Classroom for high school students and SEAmester at Sea for college students.

Elizabeth Heaston

Birthdate: 6/2/77
Hometown: Richland, Washington
School: Willamette University
Family: mom, Suzanne; dad, Dale;
sister, Karen (18)
Hobbies: soccer, my sorority (Alpha Chi
Omega), teaching swimming lessons

I never imagined myself playing football—soccer had been my entire life. I was recruited out of high school to play a defensive position at what was becoming a women's soccer powerhouse: Willamette University in Salem, Oregon. But in the fall of 1997, the nationally ranked Willamette Bearcats football team was in desperate need of a regular placekicker, and before I knew what was happening, I became a two-sport athlete and the talk of the sports world.

"If your dreams are worth it, so are the sacrifices."

– Elizabeth

How fate placed me in this position really began the year before. The starting placekicker, Gordon Thompson, had sustained a serious injury, and as the 1997 season began, he was still recovering. The Bearcat kicking game was inconsistent, and its staff was at a loss for solutions. They had asked some members of the men's soccer team to play the position, but the game schedules of the men's soccer team and the football team conflicted.

Then someone thought of recruiting a women's soccer player, and when the coach (Dan Hawkins) asked who was capable of kicking, my name came up. He was aware of my abilities and success on the soccer field, but he was unsure whether these skills would transfer to football.

When Coach Hawkins first suggested that I give it a try as placekicker, I thought he was kidding. Then he asked, "So, will I see you at practice?" and the question hit me like a lightning bolt. I was going to try playing football for the Bearcats!

At the first practice, I was a bit intimidated by the new surroundings and the weight and shape of the ball. After hitting ten out of ten attempts at Point After Touchdowns (PATs), I realized that the kicking motion was the same as what had always come naturally to me while playing soccer. And because the technique I used to approach the ball worked, there was no need to change my kicking style.

After kicking practice, Coach Hawkins decided to add my name to the roster and the regular practice schedule. I soon found out how much easier soccer equipment is to wear compared to football gear. I fumbled around, trying to put on my rib protector, shoulder pads, thigh and hip pads, and so on. Just like a kid learning to tie her first pair of shoes, I had a tough time figuring out what came next. It took the team manager, the coach, and a few players to help me get all of those pads facing the right direction.

At first, I worried about the guys on the team accepting me at football practice, but they were nice and treated me like a teammate, not like an intruder. Because they were so accepting, the transition into my strange new environment was much easier.

I've always been a dedicated and disciplined soccer player, so I had no problem working hard to learn the game of football. Each day after soccer practice, I'd hustle over to the football field and work with Gordon and

Elizabeth makes history while playing football for Willamette University.

the rest of the offense on PATs, field goals, and game situations. I believe that if you want something badly enough, you have to be willing to work hard to make it happen. I really wanted to succeed in my new position, so I told myself that I'd do whatever it would take.

Coach Hawkins decided that on October 18, I should officially suit up for a game against my school's arch rival, Linfield College. Turns out, it was a home game for both the women's soccer and the football teams. After my soccer match (our team won), I grabbed my soccer bag with one hand and my football uniform with the other and ran to my parents' van. Journalists and photographers trailed behind me as I made my way to McCulloch Football Stadium. Putting on a football uniform within the confines of a van racing to the stadium was an experience I'll never forget!

I arrived midway through the first quarter. Our team was ahead by thirteen points. Kicking in his first game since his injury, Gordon had already scored two field goals and an extra point. For the next fifteen minutes, I dodged the media and tried to focus on the game. Willamette got another touchdown, and it was time for the placekicker to go for the extra point. Instead of heading onto the field, Gordon ran up to me and shouted, "Liz, Liz, you're on!"

Stunned, I grabbed my helmet, fastened the chin strap, and ran onto the field. The crowd erupted in cheers.

I tried to focus on the job I had to do, while the scene I had visualized countless times during my mental-practice sessions (which I did regularly to calm my nerves and replace on-the-field time I couldn't get because of soccer) unfolded before me. I lined up in position and nodded to signal that I was ready.

The ball was snapped; I began my approach, planting my cleats into the turf. I saw the ball, felt my foot make solid contact with it, and watched as it sailed over the crossbar and through the uprights in what seemed like slow motion. I earned the extra point, but more important, I made history and changed the game of football forever.

I didn't really feel nervous until I got to the sidelines. Then the enormity of what had seemed like such a simple act hit me:

I was the first woman ever to play and score in a college football game. Later in the game, I kicked another extra point, and we beat Linfield 27–0.

What happened after that was amazing: I became an instant celebrity. For an entire week, I lived that defining moment every single second of every day. Each evening, I'd stop by the sports information office to pick up the piles of messages from people wanting interviews; then first thing in the morning I'd be on the phone arranging them.

I had to be up at 3 A.M., wearing my jersey and helmet for the *CBS Morning News* and NBC's *Today* because the interviews were broadcast live on the East Coast. People seemed to forget that I was still a student and an athlete playing on two teams— I had a full load of classes, plus soccer and football practice. I had anticipated a little attention, but nothing *this* big. I must have given at least twenty-five interviews in the first week alone. Luckily, it didn't take long for the excitement to die down.

Notoriety is a funny thing—you can be glorified one day and shot down the next, which is what happened to me. I made my only other appearance for the Bearcats at our next home game, where we played against Southern Oregon.

I arrived late after a soccer match and was standing on the sidelines in my football jersey and jeans, not expecting to play that day. Coach Hawkins pulled me aside when the team was walking to the locker room at halftime and asked, "Why aren't you in full uniform?"

I ran to the locker room and suited up. Gordon had missed two extra points in the first half, so the next two times we scored, the coach put me in. I was nervous, and I ended up trying too hard. I missed both PATs that I attempted, but we still won 41–27.

My unsuccessful performance landed me in the "Loser Column" in *Sports Illustrated,* just weeks after I'd been hailed for making history. The guys on the team were really angry about this, and they even threatened to write to the magazine in my defense (it was like having a bunch of big brothers looking out for me). I didn't let the magazine's opinion get me down because

I wasn't playing football for fame or notoriety; I was doing it because I wanted to help the team.

How I got started:

During the 1997 season, my college football team was in desperate need of a placekicker—it turned out to be me. This led to further opportunities, such as public speaking.

Accomplishments:

In soccer, I was team captain, an honorable mention All-American, and All-Conference (three years). My accomplishments in football include playing varsity and being the first woman to play and score in a college football game—I'm even featured in a display in the College Football Hall of Fame. I'm active in my sorority, too, as vice president (education), house manager, and warden for the Conduct of Standards and Revisions Board.

How I stay motivated:

I know that goals don't just happen—you can reach them only through hard work and perseverance. This knowledge helps me push myself harder.

My future:

I'm majoring in biology, and my goal is to become an optometrist.

I wouldn't trade the ups and downs of my season as a football player for anything. You don't get many chances in life to make history, so I decided that I should live the moment to the fullest. I did everything I could to make the most of that time.

As a result of my experience on the football field, I discovered that it's a lot easier to take a risk when you know that people are behind you. No matter what I do—football, soccer, whatever—I'm fortunate to have a great support system and cheering section. My friends, family, sorority sisters, and teammates have all been very encouraging and proud of me. I know they'll always stand by me.

Now I talk to kids about my experiences and the importance of believing in themselves. I've heard from many young women who want to play football but haven't been given the opportunity because their coaches won't put them on the roster. I believe that if someone has the talent, she should get a chance to play. I got my chance, and look what happened!

Go Exploring

Great Women in Sports by Anne Janette Johnson (Detroit: Visible Ink Press, 1996). This book is a tribute to 150 champion female athletes, from Olympians to professionals. Competitors profiled include such instrumental figures as Michelle Kwan, Chris Evert, and Wilma Rudolph.

Playing in a New League by Sara Gogol (Indianapolis: Master's Press, 1998). If you're interested in learning more about female sports figures who broke ground, check out this book, which tells the story of the athletes, coaches, and other people who helped create the American Basketball League. This professional league enabled a team of female basketball players to compete for the first time before American fans, forever changing the face of this professional sport.

Just Sports for Women Web Site
http://www.justwomen.com
This site features the most up-to-date information about women's athletics, including college, professional, extreme, and Olympic sports. In addition to news, scores, and standings, it has features on women athletes, chat rooms, advice from professionals, and a list of the best current women's sports books.

Melissa Buhl
---- BMX & Mountain Bike Racer ----

Birthdate: 1/25/82
Hometown: Chandler, Arizona
School: Corona del Sol High School
Family: mom, Cheryl; dad, Bill;
brother, Justin (18)
Hobbies: weight lifting, movies,
concerts, hanging out with friends

I f you've never seen a BMX (Bicycle Motocross) race, you don't know what you're missing. Imagine a bunch of bikers on a dirt track, riding furiously, performing amazing jumps and tricks (otherwise known as "getting air"), maneuvering around obstacles, and even cutting each other off as they race to the finish line. It's a fast, aggressive sport, but I love every minute of it!

When I first started BMX racing, I competed against girls and boys. I didn't beat the guys at first, but once I started winning, they didn't take it gracefully. Some had a real problem losing against a girl.

Today, I'm a much stronger racer, and the guys have changed their attitude toward me. Now I get a lot more respect. After seven years of racing, I can say that, for the most part, the guys I compete with accept and respect me as a rider, not as a "girl" rider.

- - - - - - - -

When a girl first starts competing in BMX, she can jump right in and sign up to race "Girl" (this is girls-only and one step below professional racing); or she can start out as a "Novice," which is coed. If you race Novice, you compete until you earn enough wins to move up to "Intermediate," which is also coed. After winning enough times, you qualify to move up to Girl. And when you're ready for stiffer competition (and are at least fifteen years old), you can turn pro. Currently, there's only one professional BMX level for female riders: Girl Pro.

> "Being confident and aware of your abilities calms you down. It's the first step toward winning."
> – Melissa

Although I knew that girls at the pro level never raced against guys, part of me wondered if this would ever change. In fact, when I was at the 1998 BMX Nationals in El Paso, Texas, my team manager, Pat Blackburn, brought up this issue to me. Little did I know that an unexpected turn of events would put an end to our speculation.

When I arrived at the BMX Nationals in May of 1998 to race Girl Pro, I didn't see many girls, and I began to wonder if I'd get the opportunity to ride. Turns out, only three girls had registered, and there had to be at least four competitors for the race to happen. According to the rule book, if there are less than four girls, the Girl Pros may be bumped up to A Pro, the starting pro level for guys (the next level up is AA Pro, which is the elite class).

The other two female riders didn't want to race A Pro, so they packed up their gear and went home. Pat and I discussed what I should do. His advice was: "Right on! You get to race pro guys!" He said I would be the first girl in the history of the American Bicycle Association (ABA) to race A Pro with guys, and this was too great of an opportunity to pass up.

Still, I had my doubts.

Later that day, I was sitting around with a few of the pro guys and several ABA staff members. They were all talking about how cool it would be if I decided to race with the guys. I was reluctant, but talking with everyone made me realize that the race might be fun.

This sport has made me a more carefree, confident person, and my training has helped me understand how important it is to take chances and risks. As I thought about the competition, I asked myself, "What have you got to lose?" I decided to go for it!

Saturday morning, May 9, was race day. When I arrived at the track, a few people said, "Hey, Melissa, no girls showed up, so it looks like you won't be racing this weekend, huh?"

I replied, "I'm going to race A Pro," like it was no big deal. Everyone seemed to get a kick out of my reply. I don't know who was more surprised by the decision, them or me.

At the start of the race, I didn't feel as nervous as usual. The guys were all supportive, and there was no pressure because no one expected anything of me. I just wanted to get out there and race the way I always did—smooth and aggressive. (This means I go through the course aggressively, but without getting all "squirrelly" and losing control.) Because all BMX riders—male or female—are aggressive when they compete, I knew this race was basically no different than others I'd been in. I told myself to stay focused on what I had to do and have fun.

Melissa practices at the local track in Chandler, Arizona.

In BMX, you race on total points earned in the *motos* (qualifying heats), with the best finishers advancing to *mains* (finals). The track in El Paso was long with a few big *doubles* (a double is a pair of hills or a dirt mound with a dip in between for taking off to perform a jump; big doubles means the mounds are far apart).

I had on my clipless shoes, which attach to the pedals so my feet don't slip, and my leathers, which are special pants worn by BMX racers. My long-sleeved jersey sported my sponsors' logos (I represent Fort McDowell Casino and Jalapeno Bikes).

Usually, it's a good idea to give your bike the once-over before a race, checking the tire pressure and making sure the parts are tight. But because I always keep my bike well-tuned, I didn't have to check anything. I just put on my full face helmet and riding gloves (all BMX riders are required to wear this type of protective gear in every race), then prepared for the start.

During a race, you have to think really fast. Other racers might bump you or try to cut you off to·reach the finish line. If someone throws an elbow or moves in your direction, you have to decide whether to back off or keep riding aggressively. If someone crashes in front of you, you must quickly figure out where to go—there's no time to hesitate. It's almost like speeding in a car and having to decide to either brake or swerve to avoid an accident. Sometimes you end up losing control of your bike and crashing.

How I got started:

When I was a little kid on training wheels, I'd ride so fast that my bike would tip sideways, and one set of wheels would fly off the ground. I used to come into the house in tears because my knees were bleeding. Now getting cut, scraped, and covered with dirt is no big deal to me. I was nine when I first became interested in Bicycle Motocross. A neighbor kid raced, and I'd go to the BMX track with him. I thought it looked like so much fun that I decided to give it a try.

Accomplishments:

1998: ABA #2 Pro Woman in BMX racing; Junior National Champion of the National Off-Road Bicycle Association (NORBA) for downhill mountain bike racing; seventh place, World Championships for downhill mountain bike racing. 1997: Amateur National Age Group Champion (15-year-olds) for BMX racing.

How I stay motivated:

I hate to lose and love to win, and this motivates me when I race. I want to be the best at what I do, so I think about this as I prepare to ride.

My future:

My goal is to continue as a BMX and mountain bike racer, while traveling the world. There are so many opportunities in my sport, and being involved in two aspects of biking may open even more doors for me. I also plan to attend college.

Whenever I'm waiting for a race to start, I try to stay calm by visualizing a good ride (visualization gives me a mental edge). My trainer, Bob Mathews, likes to say, "See it, believe it, perform it." I repeat this phrase over and over in my mind, picturing myself far ahead of the other riders.

The race began, and thoughts flew through my mind. I considered what was coming up next on the track and what choices I needed to make. I always have to be ready to make split-second decisions about how to best approach the *berms* (banked turns), how to hit the jumps, and how to out-maneuver the other riders.

In the first moto, I passed one guy in the first turn, and another in the second turn. I ended up placing third.

During the second moto, I was in fourth place when I suddenly hit some soft dirt, "slid out" (lost traction), and crashed. Chris Luna, one of the pros from Arizona, accidentally ran over me after my wipeout. He felt bad and took the time to apologize, but I hardly noticed; I just jumped back on my bike, trying to get ahead of him. I wasn't quick enough, though, and ended up one point away from qualifying for mains.

After the race, all of the other riders thought I'd qualified for mains and were happy for me. I was disappointed I didn't actually qualify, but I felt good about my performance. People came up to me and told me how impressed they were that I'd raced with the guys. I even received compliments from some of the spectators. All of this support really motivated me.

Thanks to this sport, I've made some close friends who have taught me about professionalism and confidence. But the best thing about BMX racing is that it's so fun. Nothing else in my life matches the intensity of racing. I love the pace, the crowd, the excitement, the thrill. Even though I wipe out and get scraped up sometimes, I enjoy every race.

Go Exploring

American Bicycle Association (ABA)
P.O. Box 718
Chandler, AZ 85244
(602) 961-1903
http://www.ababmx.com

ABA, the national sanctioning body for BMX racing, establishes the rules of racing and organizes qualifying events for riders to advance to the next competitive level. They host championship competitions for amateurs and professional racers.

National Bicycle League (NBL)
3958 Brown Park Drive, Suite D
Hilliard, OH 43026
(614) 777-1625
http://www.nbl.org

NBL is the first organization to bring together local and state BMX associations, sanctioning over 3,000 races per year. The league is dedicated to promoting a fun and healthy racing environment for riders.

Beth Rodden
-------------- Rock Climber --------------

Birthdate: 5/30/80
Hometown: Davis, California
School: University of California, Davis
Family: mom, Linda; dad, Robb; brother, David (21); dog, Steffi (10—the love of my life!)
Hobbies: Ping-Pong, hanging out with friends, going out for sundaes, surfing the Internet

I t was just after noon on July 3, 1998, when my friend Vic and I walked up to "the rock." We were at Donner Summit in Lake Tahoe, California, facing a rock-climbing route known as Warp Factor. This steep, overhanging granite cliff ascends about 50 feet.

Vic was going to be my *belayer*, the person who stands at the base of the cliff working the rope that's attached to the climber. Vic's job was to let rope out, or take it in, to match my progress up the slope. A belayer must always be ready to take action if a climber falls.

The sun shone, and the temperature hovered around 85 degrees. Most people would have considered it too hot to climb, but not me. If it's cold, I can't seem to get fully warmed up, and my freezing fingers don't feel as strong. I climb much better in the heat, wearing a T-shirt and using chalk to dry my hands when they sweat.

> "To make it to the top, you must be willing to overcome your fears and doubts."
>
> – Beth

A few days before I climb, I review every detail over and over in my mind. I memorize all of the moves, replaying them like a movie in my head. I see my hand positioning for each hold, and I know by heart each foot placement, body movement, and breathing sequence. This helps boost my confidence and mentally prepares me for the climb.

Because my ascent that day was for fun, not competition, I wasn't under intense pressure. Another friend of mine, Dan, who's a photographer, had come along to take pictures of my ascent. Vic, Dan, and I drank some soda, then meandered to the base of the cliff. I was a little nervous, but in general, I felt good. Before a climb, we always say, "The worst that can happen is you fall," and this little joke somehow helps break the tension.

Before ascending, I usually review the route in my mind. But at this time, I didn't because I thought that the climb wasn't going to be my *redpoint attempt*. When you redpoint, you completely ascend a very difficult climbing route from bottom to top (after having trained on the route one or more times), without assistance or hanging on the rope. I figured that my second try later the same day would be my redpoint attempt because by then the route would be fresh in my mind.

I laced up my climbing shoes, then dipped my hands in my chalk bag to dry off the sweat. I took a deep breath and approached the first handhold, where I would get a grip on the rock.

Dan called out, "Let me know when you're ready to go!"

I shouted back, "I'm ready, but this isn't my redpoint attempt!"

At first, I felt groggy and slow as I climbed, but it didn't take long for my adrenaline to kick in. Soon I was completely focused on the rock. I love the sensation of being high up and away from all of life's complications. I can leave my worries on the ground far below.

The goal in rock climbing is to conserve your energy throughout the climb, so you can make it to the top. You have to block out the pain and urge yourself to keep going.

The first six moves of this particular climb were extremely difficult, and when I moved through them, I didn't feel as good as I'd hoped. As always, my entire body strained to stay on the rock. My fingers grasped the handholds, my feet were wedged in the footholds, and my stomach helped to maintain body tension.

With sheer determination, I grunted and groaned until I finally reached my first *rest point.* (These are places on the climbing route where you can position your body to take a rest.) Once I got there, I realized that pausing too long would waste more energy than just moving right through the next phase of the route. The hardest challenge was just ahead, and I yelled down to Vic, "Okay, Vic, here I go!"

From my practice climbs on Warp Factor, I knew that the next phase of the route would require lots of finger strength and forearm endurance. On any climb, I reach a point where the sensation of the blood rushing to my forearms is so intense that my arms fail me. When this happens, I push myself to keep going, but sometimes I fall or need to rest on the rope. I realized that I had to get through the next ten moves on the route quickly, or else the steepness of the climb and the small handholds (which were hard to grip) would tax my forearms too much. I managed to get through these ten moves, but the two hardest moves of the entire route still lay ahead.

For me, climbing is not only a physical challenge but also a mental one. I need to have courage to face a hard move or a potentially big fall. If I stop to wonder if I've trained hard enough or if I'm good enough, I lose my concentration and put myself at risk. I can't afford to give in to self-doubt when I'm climbing.

Beth demonstrates her climbing skills.

I reached a small break in the route, where I had a good hold with my right hand and a so-so hold with my left. This enabled me to chalk my left hand, relieving some of the fatigue in that arm. Then, without even thinking about it, I reached for the next hold with my left hand but couldn't get a good grip; I moved on instinct, continuing upward, without letting go or hanging on the rope. I could hear my friends shouting, "Come on, Beth!"

I got through two more handholds successfully. At this point, I started thinking, "Just one more move and you're there." Resting for a moment, I rehearsed the last move in my head: "Throw out with your right hand, hold tight, move your feet, and get that left hand on the handhold quickly." I yelled down to Vic, letting him know that I was going for it.

How I got started:

In the fall of 1994, my dad took me to the local indoor climbing gym, and I fell in love with the movement of climbing and the challenge of figuring out how to approach the rock wall. It captured my interest like nothing else ever had.

Accomplishments:

I was named the 1998 Junior National Champion (girls ages 18–19) and the 1998 Junior International Invitational Challenge Champion. Currently, I'm the #1 ranked competitive female climber in the U.S. (adult division).

How I stay motivated:

Every now and then, the pressure of climbing gets to me, and negative thoughts like "I can't" creep into my brain. But I know that if I simply relax and get some perspective, the word *can* comes right back into my head. If all else fails, I rent a movie like *Rocky* or *Jerry Maguire,* which helps me get excited about facing a challenge again.

My future:

I'm considering a career in business or maybe exercise science, but I haven't decided yet. As for climbing, I want to compete for a few more years and then focus on harder routes, both indoors and outdoors. I'd like to travel to places like Australia and Thailand to experience more rock-climbing challenges.

I reached with my right hand toward what turned out to be a *bad edge* (a horizontal hold that has very little surface area, making it hard to grip). There was no turning back now, though.

I heard Dan shout, "Fight hard, Rodden!" Somehow this triggered some sort of beast inside me—I've never held on so tight in my life!

I knew that I had to keep moving, or else fall from exhaustion. As my left hand went into motion to reach for the next hold, I yelled, gripped with all of my might, and lunged. This would be my moment of truth. Would I make it?

I reached the *finishing hold* (the final one) and felt an amazing sense of accomplishment. From my perch high above the ground, I signaled to Vic that I was ready to be lowered back down.

As I watched the ground getting closer, I realized I'd done something I'd always hoped to do: I'd completed a *5.13 route* (a route with a high level of difficulty). When I finished the route for the first time without assistance (a redpoint ascent), I felt as if I'd made it into an elite class that had always seemed beyond my reach. For me, this was like taking the ultimate step in rock climbing—I'd moved away from the common climbing field into a group of a select few.

I gained a lot of confidence from this experience, so I no longer get as anxious before rock-climbing competitions. I think my new sense of calm is the result of experience. I'd never considered myself a strong outdoor climber, but redpointing Warp Factor proved otherwise.

I've learned how important it is to push yourself and strive for excellence. If I want to achieve something, I know it won't necessarily be easy, but I'll never settle for a so-so effort. I'll give 100 percent!

Go Exploring

The Climber's Handbook by Garth Hattingh (Mechanicsburg, PA: Stackpole Books, 1998). The full-color pictures in this book convey the fun and challenge of rock climbing. You'll find information on competitive climbing, indoor wall climbing, bouldering, sport climbing, Alpine (snow and ice) climbing, expeditions, and more.

Rock Climbing: A Trailside Guide by Don Mellor (New York: W. W. Norton & Co., 1997). Filled with color photos of equipment and climbers in action, this book is a comprehensive guide to climbing—including the history of the sport, how to get started, basic movements, knot tying, rappelling, safety precautions, and injury prevention.

 Climbing Magazine
P.O. Box 420235
Palm Coast, FL 32142
1-800-829-5895
http://www.climbing.com

This magazine includes features on amazing climbing experiences, as well as photos, technical tips for climbers, interviews, news, and information about upcoming events.

Rock and Ice Magazine
603A S. Broadway
Boulder, CO 80303
1-877-ROCKICE (1-877-762-5423)
http://www.rockandice.com

Rock and Ice includes features, technical tips, and product information for mountaineers and climbers. Log onto their Web site to check out the current issue, or join the *Rock and Ice* Correspondents Network for access to fellow climbers.

Anastasia Krivosta

----------- Judo Competitor -----------

Birthdate: 4/30/82
Hometown: Smithtown, New York
School: Smithtown High School
Family: mom, Elaine; dad, George; brothers,
Paul Jacob (12) and Jason Alexander (19 months)
Hobbies: track and field, baton, music,
volunteering at a nursing home

Have you ever done something that just felt so right? This is how I feel about judo. It's hard to put into words how much this sport means to me. Some people say that when you fall in love, it just hits you. I guess you could say that I "fell in love" with judo. When I win, I want to laugh, cry, and shout at the same time.

Judo was developed by a Japanese schoolteacher, Dr. Jigaro Kano, in 1882. The word *judo* itself helps explain the philosophy behind the sport. The first part of the word, *ju,* means "gentle" or "giving"; the second part, *do,* means "way." Together, judo stands for "gentle way," a principle that has become the foundation of my life. I try to live up to this principle inside and outside the *dojo* (training hall).

Judo comes from an earlier martial art known as jujitsu. In judo, you use quick movements and leverage to throw your opponent. It's a nonviolent sport because the focus is on self-defense, discipline, humility, and honor. You rely on "maximum efficient use of power," which means that you use your opponent's force against her (or him).

I compete locally, nationally, and internationally in both the junior and senior levels. I placed fifth at the 1998 Senior National Championships, which is a qualifying tournament for both the Olympic Team and the World Championship Team. Although I finished out of the medals (I wasn't among the top three winners), I earned a spot on the Junior Team U.S.A. The Junior Team (for competitors under age sixteen) helps athletes prepare for future competition in the Olympic Games.

> "If you really want something, don't stop until you get it, and don't let anyone tell you that you can't."
>
> – Anastasia

Earning a spot on the Junior Team is my greatest win to date. I was given the opportunity to attend the first Youth World Championships, an athletic competition held in Moscow in July 1998. The International Olympic Committee (IOC) sponsored these games, and athletes from all over the world participated.

The trip to Moscow marked the first time I ever traveled out of the United States, as well as my first time competing in a tournament without having my dad there. My dad is not only my *sensei* (teacher) but also my coach and trainer. I'm grateful for all he has taught me, especially dedication and persistence. (This means that I learn and train, and I learn and train some more, and then some more!)

My dad has earned black belts in judo—he holds the rating of expert. A Japanese saying on one of my dad's black belts translates this way: "Form becomes emptiness, emptiness becomes form." I interpret this to mean that you must practice over and over, until the moves become second nature. In a judo match, everything happens fast, and you don't have time to stop and think. You have to rely on your instincts, but you must develop your instincts so they serve you well.

While preparing for the Youth World Championships, I kept thinking about how much I wanted to win and make my family proud. I couldn't believe that I would be competing in such a far-off place.

On the day of my departure, my family drove me to the airport, where I would board a plane to Chicago to meet up with the staff in charge of Olympic training. We arrived at the airport early, so I had a lot of time to think about what it would be like to be away from home. As my boarding time crept closer, I began to get nervous and scared.

My teammate, Mike Merkovich, noticed how anxious I was. He started teasing me, saying that if I didn't compete well in Moscow, the team might not let me on the plane going home. He said that I would have to walk across Alaska to get back. This made me laugh, and I relaxed a little. When it was time to leave, I said good-bye to my family and tried to focus on the challenges ahead . . . not on what I was leaving behind.

Once we arrived in Chicago, we filled out a bunch of forms and received our visas for traveling abroad. We also were given our U.S.A. team clothing, which we would wear to Russia and to the opening ceremony of the championships. That night in Chicago, we worked out and ate a pasta dinner.

Next, we boarded a plane headed to Frankfurt, Germany, and from there to Russia. I sat alone, worrying about so many things. The ride felt long and lonely to me. I missed my family, and I kept trying to imagine where they were and what they were doing. Traveling without them, I felt as if I had to be grown-up and responsible, but my mind was filled with doubt.

I feared that I might not make my weight (you have to weigh in at or under the weight division in which you're contending). I was also afraid that I *would* make my weight (which meant that I'd really have to compete!). Part of me wanted nothing more than to compete, and another part of me wished I didn't have to. I wondered how tough my competitors would be and what it would feel like to face them on the mat. What if I didn't do well? What if I disappointed everyone?

I was also apprehensive about what Russia would be like. I'm proud to be a third-generation American, but my heritage is Russian. Here I was, the first person in my family to return to our homeland. Because I don't know how to speak Russian, I felt anxious about communicating with the people I would meet.

When the plane landed in Moscow, I started to get excited—not to mention more nervous. As we got off the plane, we were met by children who handed us flowers and balloons. A little girl came up to me and asked me my name. She spoke English (what a relief for me!). I told her my name was Anastasia, and she told me hers was, too. I soon discovered that Anastasia is a very common name in Russia.

The team traveled by bus to the Olympic Village, the buildings that house those participating in the games. People who stay here—athletes, coaches, medical personnel, support staff, and interpreters—come from all over the world. At the village, I saw many people attired in traditional Russian dress, which looked very festive. I loved seeing the type of clothing that my great-grandparents might have worn.

I learned that I would be staying in an apartment (which consisted of a living room, bedrooms, and a bathroom) with the girls fencing team from the United States, and that I would be sharing a bedroom with my junior team coach. After we had settled in, we got busy with our training. We practiced every day for about two hours, even on the days we competed.

In between training and competitions, we had time to do some sightseeing. We visited Red Square and St. Basil's Cathedral, a church more magnificent than I ever could have imagined. We looked at many other historical churches and buildings, which were elaborate and ornate. The *kuplas* (upside-down onion-shaped domes) on the churches were breathtaking—so shiny, colorful, and bright. We have kuplas on some churches in America, but they're nothing like the ones that I saw in Russia. In Russia, the kuplas are larger than

Anastasia *(right)* practices judo throws with her brother Paul Jacob.

life, and I just kept thinking how proud I was that my family had originally come from this amazing place.

We shopped on the city's oldest street, where I bargained for a Russian fur hat for my dad and picked out a scarf for my grandma. Everywhere I went, I brought candy and U.S.A. flag pins to trade with people, and I gave gum to the children I met. They thanked me, saying my name in Russian. I even got to eat traditional Russian cuisine, including caviar and herring.

This trip made me miss and appreciate the comforts of home. In Russia, the showers had very little water pressure, and the toilet paper was brown and rough. We had to use bottled water for drinking, washing, and brushing our teeth. I realized how many things in my life I take for granted.

How I got started:

Growing up, I admired my dad so much, and I wanted to do everything he did. I watched him practice judo, so naturally I had to get on the mat, too. At the age of five, I started training at the Smithtown YMCA Judo Club.

Accomplishments:

1998: Fifth place, Senior National Championships. 1997: Gold medalist, U.S. National Ladder Tournament; silver and bronze medalist, U.S. Junior National Invitational; gold medalist, U.S. National Junior Olympics; gold medalist, New York Mayor's Cup. 1996: Gold medalist, U.S. National Junior Olympics; gold medalist, U.S. Junior National Championships; gold medalist, New York Mayor's Cup; New York Junior & Senior Champion. 1995: Gold medalist, U.S. Junior International Invitational; second place, American Canadian International; bronze medalist, U.S. National Junior Olympics.

How I stay motivated:

I watch other competitors at their matches to get a sense of their technique. I also listen to my dad and other judo coaches. My mom is my #1 fan, and she helps me focus, stay organized, and reach my goals.

My future:

Someone once told me, "Everyone has the will to win—you must have the will to *train* to win." I have my sights set on making the next Olympic judo team and going for the gold, and I'll train hard to reach this goal. I also want a good education, and I hope to go to college someday.

The Russian people were friendly, especially when they saw my name on my credentials (they must have figured out that I was of Russian descent). When I competed, the crowd chanted my last name, "Krivosta! Krivosta!" The people cheered for me during all of my matches, with one exception: When I competed against a girl from the republic of Russia, they clapped and hollered for her.

The most fun I had on my trip was being a part of the opening ceremonies of the championships. To me, it was like the Olympics, and I felt so incredibly proud to be one of the athletes. As I sat there with the other members of the American team, wearing official clothing, I couldn't believe this was happening to me. There I was, representing the United States, surrounded by representatives of 130 other nations. I took dozens and dozens of pictures, so I'd never forget that special moment.

The judo competitions were held outside the Olympic Village at *Druzhba,* the Universal Sports Hall. The morning of my tournament, I woke up with one thought running through my mind: I wanted to win, or place second or third. I felt nervous and sick to my stomach.

My first match of the day started in the early afternoon, and everything went well. I won the match against a girl from Turkmenistan. Next I had to beat Severine Pesch, from Germany, to earn the right to fight for third place.

They announced my match. I knew that Severine was a strong contender, and I'd have to use all of my wits and strength to win. Right away, I received a penalty for stalling because I was ducking under her arm to avoid her high, dominating grip.

The next few minutes were all about technique. I almost threw Severine twice, and she almost got me in a choke hold. At one point, she twisted my shoulder and was applying pressure to it; I was in a lot of pain. We were equally matched, but when the clock ran out, I learned that I'd lost the match by one-eighth of a point. That was it for me—no more matches and no medal.

I felt sad and disappointed. I'd wanted to be the first U.S. female judo player to earn a medal at the first Youth World Championships. I believed that I'd let everybody down, and I began to question my performance in the match. I wondered where I'd gone wrong and what I could have done better.

Later, with the help of my coach and teammates, I came to realize that I'd done my best. I was pleased that I placed ninth in the world at my first international competition overseas.

There will always be a next time. My dream is to become an Olympic athlete, and I have the desire and dedication to make this dream come true. I'll keep improving my skills until each match is better than the last. I know that giving something my best shot is what truly makes me a winner.

Go Exploring

Martial Arts for Women: A Practical Guide by Jennifer Lawler (Hartford, CT: Turtle Press, 1998). This reference book, for girls and women who are interested in martial arts, includes information on the different forms of martial arts, how to find a class, safety gear, and injury prevention. You'll also find advice on defining your goals and developing a winning spirit.

A Woman's Guide to Martial Arts by Monica McCabe-Cardoza (Woodstock, NY: The Overlook Press, 1998). This book of basics describes different types of martial arts and the pros and cons of each. You'll learn about finding a class, martial arts etiquette, and ways to overcome beginner's fears.

U.S. Judo Association
21 N. Union Boulevard
Colorado Springs, CO 80909
(719) 633-7750
http://www.csprings.com/usja

As the national governing body for judo, this association provides information about clubs across the country, sanctions competitive events, and encourages participation in the martial arts.

Sarah Jacobson

---------------- Fossil Hunter ----------------

Birthdate: 6/9/83
Hometown: Urbana, Illinois
School: Urbana High School
Family: mom, Linda; dad, Russ; sisters,
Heather (19) and Sharon (17)
Hobbies: volleyball,
horseback riding, softball

I was never all that interested in dinosaurs, but my dad is a paleontologist, and I couldn't help hearing about his work. He was so enthusiastic when he talked about the fossil digs he'd been on that I decided to see for myself what fossil hunting was like.

You're probably wondering what a teenage girl could find interesting about spending the summer crouched over a bunch of fossils in the scorching sun. But it was more than interesting; it was amazing!

The first dig I went on was in South Dakota, in the summer of 1996. My dad and his coworker, Steve Sroka, led the expedition. Because my parents thought I might get bored, they only signed me up for a one-week trip. I had so much fun that the time flew by. The following summer, they let me return for three weeks.

"It's tough trying something new that pushes you to become emotionally and physically stronger. But it's worth it!"

– Sarah

I arrived in South Dakota in July 1997, ready to begin my second field expedition. The group (about twenty people total) stayed on a ranch with the family who lived there. Because my dad and Steve were in charge of the dig, the three of us got to stay in a cabin, but everybody else pitched tents next to the main house.

The ranch was located on a wide expanse of South Dakota frontier, which to some people might look dead and ugly. But to my eyes, the landscape was breathtakingly beautiful. Whenever I looked at the flatlands that stretched before the horizon, I could almost see dinosaurs roaming around.

The first week of the dig was exciting because everyone was full of energy and felt optimistic about what we might find. Each morning, we were up with the sun, ready to get out and start digging by 7 A.M. It was always a wild ride driving to the sites; the vehicles jerked over miles of bumpy off-road terrain, making us feel like we were in an *Indiana Jones* movie. We'd drive as far as we could, then hike to the digging area, known as the Hell Creek Formation.

Sixty-five million years ago, dinosaurs wandered this spot amidst lush vegetation, rivers, and streams. Now the site is nothing but layers of sun-baked rock and dirt.

It wasn't unusual for the temperature to climb over 100 degrees. While working outdoors in the blazing South Dakota sun, it was essential to wear the proper gear. To protect ourselves, we wore sunglasses and hats, and we drank plenty of water to prevent dehydration. There was hardly any shade, so the only comfort from the heat came from the occasional passing cloud or gust of hot wind.

The ground on which we worked was harsh. We wore thick hiking boots and pants to protect ourselves from prickly pears and bug bites. The combination of harsh elements and hard work left me exhausted. By the end of each day, I was so tired that all I wanted to do was collapse, and my legs felt as if they couldn't take another step. The vehicle

Sarah *(left)* and a couple of her fellow fossil hunters prepare a specimen at the Hell Creek Formation in South Dakota.

that took us back to the ranch each day was definitely a sight for sore eyes after long hours in the hot sun.

As the days wore on, it became harder to get up early to face the heat and meticulous work. Some days—after several hours of sitting in the blazing sun, sweating up a storm, and digging away in the dirt—I started to feel totally exhausted, and I almost didn't want to go on. But I tried to stay positive and focus on what an amazing opportunity this was for me. Here I was, getting a chance to handle the bones of creatures that had been dead for millions of years.

One day, I forgot my hat and didn't drink enough water. I learned firsthand how strongly the heat can affect a person. I couldn't think clearly, and I started to feel dizzy and queasy. Luckily, Steve gave me an extra hat, and I felt a lot better after I found some shade, drank water, and rested. Then it was back to digging.

How I got started:

I became curious about my dad's work (paleontology), and I wanted to learn about it myself.

Accomplishments:

Over the course of the two summers I spent in South Dakota, we found remains from several different types of dinosaurs. When I stop to think about it, it's pretty amazing that people can actually search for dinosaur bones, dig them up, and hold them in their hands!

How I stay motivated:

I enjoy working with dinosaur bones, but even more, I love seeing South Dakota (one of my favorite places in the whole world) and all of the people I know and am close to there.

My future:

Although my goals don't include a career in paleontology, I do want to work with animals—*live* ones, that is. I'd like to go to college and become a veterinarian, so I can work with exotic species, either in a zoo or in the wild. My expeditions in South Dakota will help me reach these goals; the digs have taught me that it's never too early to start thinking about your future, and you must be strong enough to reach for your dreams.

We spent a lot of time at the *Hadrosaur* quarry, a site that had been discovered two years earlier. We carefully uncovered ribs, vertebrae, and other bones belonging to these duck-billed plant eaters. Another area where we dug was known as the Snake Pit, which was appropriately named since that's where we saw our first rattlesnake. Whenever we located a new bone, we looked carefully at the surrounding areas, hoping to uncover the rest of the dinosaur's body.

When we weren't excavating a specific area, we'd spend the day exploring and looking for other fossil remains. Some of the most exciting things we found were teeth, jaw bones, and skulls from ancient carnivores like the *Tyrannosaurus rex* (also known as the T-rex).

The best site we discovered was Triceratops Hill. This spot contained mammoth-sized skulls and other bones from the pre-historic *Triceratops,* a dinosaur with a huge head, three horns on its face, a bony frill around its neck, and a short tail. Nearby, we came across an area with bones scattered as far as my eyes could see.

Although I'm not a paleontologist, I was able to help prepare the specimens we excavated, a detailed and important procedure. Once you find part of a bone sticking out of the dirt, you prepare it using *Butvar* (a semipermanent glue) so that the bone doesn't fall apart. Then you continue digging until the piece is completely exposed.

Once the bone is uncovered, you use Butvar on it again and *trench* around it (dig a trench), which raises the bone onto a dirt pedestal. Next, you place layers of toilet paper on the bone, dab it with water, and *jacket* it (protect it) with a kind of plaster. After the plaster jacket dries, you carefully dig the bone loose with a *trowel* (a small shovel with a pointed tip), quickly and carefully flip the bone over, and repeat the process on the other side. The method may sound somewhat simple, but it's not. You have to be extremely careful, which is difficult when you're hunched over in the dirt.

As part of this procedure, I spent a lot of time chiseling away rock from very fragile bones. My dad and Steve were patient with me as I learned the technique. More experienced members of the field crew who had returned for their second year were helpful, too.

Believe me, it can be tiring to chip away at rock and dirt for hours, without seeming to make any progress. Add to this snakes, bugs, horseflies, and wasps, and you have a recipe for frustration! I just kept telling myself that every day of the dig had something new to offer. Who knew what we might discover?

Nature had a way of providing interesting surprises and impressive sights. On the rancher's land were areas of ground that looked dry and cracked like the rest of the landscape. But if you were to put your feet on this surface and press lightly, the terrain would jiggle like jelly. And if you pushed a bit harder, you could break the "crust" and liquid mud would ooze from the cracks. One time, my dad poked his walking stick in the mud and couldn't even find the bottom!

The summer storms of South Dakota were another source of wonder. Suddenly they'd blaze across the land, and with nothing to stop them on the open plains, they'd build to an intense level. Flashes of lightning. Hail that dented car roofs. And fierce wind. Once, a small tornado actually threw an outhouse we had built near one of the sites. The rain accompanying the wind was so heavy that the long, rocky site where we did a lot of our work was nearly washed away.

No matter how bad the storms got, they were beautiful to observe. One time, after a storm had passed, the sky was colored a shockingly bright reddish-pink. A triple rainbow arched across the sky, and lightning flashed around it. We stood outside and stared in awe.

I truly enjoy uncovering clues to the past in the middle of the beautiful South Dakota scenery. But the thing I love most about going on these digs is seeing the people I've become so close to, especially the rancher's family and the other young people on the digs. I also enjoy getting away from home and exploring another place.

I dearly love South Dakota. When I climb and hike its rocky cliffs or outcrops, I get a wonderful sensation of being daring, adventurous, and free. At the end of each day's work, I had fun cooling off in a creek, riding horses, shopping in town, or going out to eat. I've become so close to everyone on the digs that I can't wait to return to South Dakota in the future.

Some of my friends back home don't understand what I get from "digging in the dirt." They think it's sort of stupid, but I don't care. It might be easier if I just stayed home all summer and hung out, but where's the challenge in that?

Going on digs has given me the chance to find out what the earth was like before humans existed and to grow as an individual. I've learned how to get along with a wide variety of people, to be responsible and careful in high-risk situations, and to take care of myself.

All in all, the work has been exhausting but exciting. What could be more interesting than finding an ancient bone embedded in its dirt hiding place for millions of years, then uncovering this fragile piece of history for all the world to see?

Go Exploring

The Complete Idiot's Guide to Dinosaurs by Jay Stevenson, George R. McGhee, and Kevin Padian (New York: Macmillan, 1998). You'll find tons of easy-to-read information about different types of dinosaurs (including how to pronounce their names), as well as accounts of famous explorers and their discoveries. This resource is filled with fun facts about dinosaurs in books, films, and on TV, and it contains a list of the largest dinosaur displays in the country.

Dino Russ's Lair

http://www.inhs.uiuc.edu/isgsroot/dinos/dinos_home.html

Find out about previous and upcoming Hell Creek Field Expeditions at this Web site, affiliated with the Illinois State Geological Survey. You'll also find lots of links to additional sites, and information about exhibits, dinosaurs, and news in the world of paleontology.

Crystal Pakizer
-------------------- Vaulter --------------------

Birthdate: 2/11/83
Hometown: Acton, California
School: Vasquez High School
Family: mom, Debi; dad, Dan; brothers,
Brian (18) and Phillip (17)
Hobbies: horseback riding, rock climbing,
football, running, cheerleading

t's like flying! This comes closest to describing what it feels like to be a vaulter, dancing on my horse as she canters around the arena. It's so incredible to be airborne; the sensation is almost impossible to put into words.

I started riding my own horse (a trusty gelding named Sonny) at age two. In 1988, when I was five, my mom and I were invited to watch a vaulting demonstration at the 4-H Club. I was spellbound watching the horse canter around the vaulting circle, which was 15 meters in diameter. On its back the horse wore a special strap called a *vaulting surcingle* (not a saddle with stirrups). The surcingle was buckled around the horse's belly and had two hard handles attached to it; the vaulter used the handles for support when performing tricks.

> "It's normal to be hesitant when trying something different, but everyone has to start somewhere."
>
> – Crystal

The horse was guided on a lead held by a *longeur,* who controlled the horse by holding onto the *lunge line,* a long piece of cotton material attached to the horse's bridle. I was mesmerized watching the vaulter perform moves that were a beautiful blend of athleticism and grace.

The moment I first saw vaulting, I knew I had to give it a try. Every day, I asked my mom if I could do "the horse thing." She says I gave her no peace until she called the vaulting club and set up lessons.

From the very first day, I fit in and wasn't afraid to go fast or try new things. Although I had no formal dance or gymnastics training, my coach said I was a natural. The vaulting club used big draft horses, and I was so small that I had to be lifted onto their backs (I couldn't reach the handles on the surcingle by myself). I took lessons once a week, and two months later entered my first competition, bringing home two first- and two second-place ribbons.

As talented as any vaulter may be, it's only through the willingness and generosity of the horse that the sport of vaulting exists. From mount to dismount, a vaulter must consider the horse's safety to ensure her own. If the horse is uncomfortable, the vaulter will be, too. Horse and vaulter are partners—a team. As vaulters, we owe these animals our deepest gratitude and respect.

By the summer of 1990, I had become accomplished enough to qualify for the American Horse Show Association/American Vaulting Association (AHSA/AVA) National Vaulting Championships in the Trot level—the beginning point for most U.S. vaulters. In this competition, the horse trots around the ring while the vaulter performs a compulsory set of seven moves, including mounting and dismounting with no assistance. I entered three events: Individual (performing alone), Team (with a four-person team), and Pas de Deux (in pairs). Our coach increased our training schedule, so we were practicing seven days a week.

When we train, we use live horses as well as a specially made piece of equipment called a *vaulting barrel.* The barrel is padded and stationary, and it looks somewhat like the pommel horse used in gymnastics. There are two handles on top made of curved steel bars. We use it as our practice horse—it takes all of the lumps and bumps before we try any moves on a real horse. During competition, vaulters sometimes perform on the barrel, which gives the horses a rest.

At the 1990 Nationals, the barrel was set at the standard height of 4 feet (taller than I was!). The horses themselves were were up to 6 feet tall. In some photos of me from that competition, the only things showing were my legs, which were peeking out from underneath the horse, or the tips of my fingers as I stood beside the barrel and signaled high in the air for the music to start. You can't see my head or the rest of my body!

The National Championships is the largest vaulting competition in the United States. Vaulters of all ages perform compulsory and freestyle routines. Freestyle (also known as *Kür*) includes handstands, cartwheels, shoulder stands, and many other moves that the rider chooses and performs in time to music.

Although most of the other vaulters at Nationals were double and triple my age, I placed eighth and twelfth overall, and our four-person team captured the National Championship title. The most vivid memory I have of that competition isn't the moment they put the championship medal around my neck, but the middle of the competition when I lost my first tooth!

Crystal does a sidestand on her horse, Beautiful Belle.

The following year (1991), the Nationals were held in Albuquerque, New Mexico. My dad worked extra hours so our entire family could afford to attend. I entered the same three classes as I had the previous year. As an individual, I placed in the top ten and came in fourth in Pas de Deux. Plus, our four-person team won the National Championship title again. I felt pretty good about it all, especially since I was only seven years old.

I wanted nothing more than to keep training, but traveling to my lessons had become a hardship on my family. I was now training four times a week, and we had to drive about 50 miles to my lessons. My mom, who was my constant companion, "taxi driver," and "living-room coach," decided to start a vaulting club in our community. We purchased a young mare named Blue, changed her name to Belle, and began a new adventure.

Although I was competent enough to advance to the elite canter level, Belle was not. She had been a vaulting horse for only six months when we entered our first competition as members of our new club. My mom and I thought we would have to write off that entire season due to Belle's lack of experience, but to our delight and amazement, Belle turned out to be a very good vaulting horse. We placed first in almost every class, and we took many Overall titles. Still, Belle wasn't experienced enough to attend Nationals in 1992, so I had no national ranking that year.

During the next few seasons, I continued to devote a lot of time and effort to vaulting, working on my strength and form, attending clinics, and talking to judges and other coaches for any advice they were willing to spare. I watched different sports like ice skating, gymnastics, and cheerleading, looking for new and creative moves that I could apply to vaulting.

In 1993, our region (which includes Arizona, southern California, southern Nevada, and Utah) held its first regional championships. Belle and I won our first of seven consecutive regional titles. I changed her name to Beautiful Belle and continued training and competing.

I thought I had a good chance of winning the National Individual Championship title in 1995. But it didn't work out that way. The first day of the competition, I fell off Beautiful Belle and heard the audience go silent. The accident broke my arm in two places and shattered my dream of capturing the title.

Turns out, I had broken some bones in my right forearm and crushed the growth plate near my wrist. This meant the growth of my bones might be affected, leaving me with one arm permanently shorter than the other. Due to the severity of my injury, my family packed up our belongings and took me home to rest.

Until the accident, everything in my vaulting career had come easy. Now, I was scared and uncertain about how the injury might affect my future as a vaulter. This accident really gave me perspective about my sport and my life. I started to look at things in a whole new light. For the first time, I realized that my future was up to me and so was my recovery. If I was going to remain a vaulter, I'd have to take charge of my health.

The doctors I talked to had a different opinion. They advised me to quit vaulting, but I refused to give it up. Vaulting had become a regular part of my life, like waking up in the morning and brushing my teeth, and I couldn't imagine a day without it. Nothing could have kept me off my horse, so my mother wisely loaned Beautiful Belle to a neighboring club an hour and a half away.

I was determined to stay in shape, so I sneaked out at night and practiced on my vaulting barrel, cast and all. To compensate for the temporary loss of my right hand, I developed new moves using my left side. I couldn't allow my competitive spirit to give in to adversity, yet there were times when I wondered if I would ever be the vaulter I once was. When doubts like these entered my mind, I'd convince myself that with time and effort, I *would* eventually succeed. I was determined to be as good, if not better, than before.

Positive thinking prevailed. The doctors were amazed that I was able to regain my strength and range of motion so quickly, but they still said it would be best if I hung up my "vaulting shoes." I decided to prove them all wrong.

After giving myself a few more months to recuperate, I got back on Beautiful Belle again. Nothing could have made me happier. When the next competitive season began, I made my "re-debut." The judge who had witnessed my fall at Nationals gave me an encouraging smile—and all first places. I was back!

Ironically, 1996 turned out to be one of the best years of my career. The AVA had worked to get vaulting included as a demonstration event at the 1996 Summer Olympics in Atlanta, Georgia, and was selecting vaulters to represent the United States. Based on my skill, scores, character, and enthusiasm, I was chosen for the American Vaulting Association's Friendship Team. Once again, my dad worked hard to earn money so that he and my mom could join me. Performing at the Olympics as an ambassador of my sport was the experience of a lifetime, and a privilege I won't soon forget.

How I got started:

I learned about vaulting in 1988 when I was five. My mom and I attended a local vaulting demonstration, and from that day on, I was hooked.

Accomplishments:

I'm a seven-time Regional Champion, a three-time National Champion, and the only current double silver medalist in Region One (half of the West Coast). I was a member of the 1996 Olympic Friendship Team, too, which I'm really proud of.

How I stay motivated:

Two main things motivate me, besides my love of the sport: (1) the feeling of accomplishment I get when I put up new ribbons on my wall or new trophies on my dresser, and (2) the look of pride on my parents' faces.

My future:

For every goal I've reached, I have ten more to accomplish. I hope to eventually compete in Europe, and I'd also like to participate in the World Equestrian Games, an international competition for equestrian sports that aren't included in the Olympics.

When I returned home from Atlanta, I had only nine days to practice for Nationals. I knew that my competitors at Nationals had been rehearsing the whole time I was training for the Olympic demonstration, and I figured they had a better chance of winning than I did. I put in as many hours of practice as I could, and I did my best to stay optimistic.

Maybe it was due to my positive outlook or all my years of training, but the competition went great for me. The 1996 National Individual Championship title, elusive so many times, was now mine. I'd done it!

Go Exploring

The Random House Book of Horses and Horsemanship by Paula Rodenas (New York: Random House, 1991). This is an excellent resource for horse lovers; it's filled with information and wonderful full-color pictures. Learn about the history and behavior of horses, different breeds, horse care, training, riding lessons, attire, and competition (including vaulting, rodeo, polo, dressage, three-day eventing, and show jumping).

American Vaulting Association (AVA)
642 Alford Place
Bainbridge Island, WA 98110
http://www.horsenet.com/ava/

The AVA, which sanctions events and ranks vaulters based on their performance standings, publishes *Vaulting World* magazine. Their Web site offers historical information on the sport, definitions of competition levels and categories, and more.

Tara Hamilton
------------ Wakeboarder ------------

Birthdate: 1/16/82
Hometown: Lantana, Florida
School: Lakeworth Christian School
Family: mom, Nancy; dad, Tom
Hobbies: anything that's
active and fun

I was definitely the new kid on the block when I arrived at the ESPN X Games (the "Alternative" or "Extreme" Olympics) in San Diego, California, in June 1997. Not only was I young—just fifteen—but I'd been wakeboarding for only nine months.

I was as surprised as anyone else at how quickly I'd picked up this sport, working my way to such a high level of competition in less than a year. But with the help of my coach, Darin Shapiro, and the support of my family, I'd made it. I didn't know it then, but I was on the verge of a major victory.

The X Games are the Olympics for athletes involved in alternative sports. Athletes who go to the Summer X Games compete against the best in the world in extreme sports like bicycle stunt riding, aggressive in-line skating, sportclimbing, street luge, skysurfing, barefoot jumping, and my sport—wakeboarding.

Wakeboarding is basically surfing behind a boat; it's kind of like waterskiing (you're towed behind the boat by a rope), but you use a smaller version of a surfboard, instead of skis. Riders perform all kinds of cool tricks like turns, rolls, and flips by using the wake (waves created behind the boat) to launch their board in the air.

The adrenaline rush is incredible! It's hard to describe exactly how wakeboarding feels, but it's almost like you're getting ready to fly.

Imagine yourself jumping up and down on a trampoline, performing tricks while being pulled by a boat going about 20 miles per hour. This is what it's like to go wakeboarding. It's the most amazing feeling to be on the water, knowing that I can do anything.

The atmosphere at the X Games was fun but professional. It was so cool to see the city of San Diego and all of the different sites where they held the athletic events. The energy level was high, and everyone I talked to kept saying how totally excited they were.

Surprisingly, I wasn't intimidated by the competition. I told myself that the X Games were just like any other tournament and that I needed to focus on what I had to do. I tried to keep in mind how many other sporting events were going on there, so I could put my upcoming performance into perspective.

Every rider turns in an "attack sheet" to the judges at least an hour before the competition starts. This sheet shows the list of the tricks that riders will be doing in their "run" (series of tricks). Each run consists of two "passes," in which you travel the length of one side of the lake (the first pass) and then turn around and cover the other side (the second pass).

Riders are responsible for choreographing their own run. You're judged on your style (particularly on clean landings) and on how high you go into the air. I do a few tricks that other girls haven't been able to do so far, and this sets me apart from the other riders. For example, I'm still the only female ever to have performed and landed a *front flip* during competition. In wakeboarding, front flips are similar to the ones you see in gymnastics, but as the board goes sideways in the air, you have to rotate sideways yourself. Overall, I'm known for going higher into the air during runs and for having cleaner landings than other riders.

> "Confidence is at least half of everything you do."
> – Tara

As I mentally prepared myself before my run, I tried to overcome my biggest fear—falling on my first trick. If this happens, your pass is over, and you receive a "no credit."

I concentrated on each trick I planned to perform, and on blocking out the crowd and cameras. I pretended this was just another practice run, hoping I wouldn't feel too pressured. I was nervous, but I was also exhilarated and pumped up—definitely ready to go!

The boat took off. I maneuvered on the water to find the right wake for my first trick. You can tell if a wake is good by how it looks and then by the "pop" it gives you (how high it launches you into the air).

The run was going great. Some of the more difficult tricks I performed included a *raley*—where the board was behind me and my body was horizontal (kind of like Superman flying), and

Tara performs a trick on her wakeboard.

I had to bring the board back down on the water—and a *tantrum,* which is basically a back flip. I nailed each trick—until the last one of my first pass. I missed my landing and wiped out.

Despite falling, I knew I'd done well. I thought that I might have won the silver medal. I went up to Andrea Gaytan, the top female rider in the sport (who was the favorite going in), and congratulated her on winning the gold.

Then, to my amazement, the results came up and I found out that *I* had placed first. Seeing my name up there in the top position felt amazing. I'd actually won the gold medal!

Afterward, things happened fast. Cameras and interviewers surrounded me before I even had time to dry off and change into my clothes. Suddenly I was the center of attention.

For the next hour, as soon as one reporter or photographer left, someone else tracked me down, asking for a comment or quote. It was a little intimidating but fun, too.

Later, I discovered that the judges had given Andrea a no credit on one of her tricks because her landing wasn't clean. My fall and her no credit made us even, at nine tricks each. The judges decided that I rode cleaner and had a better overall performance, which is why they placed me first.

I was in a whirlwind. I felt proud, thrilled, and amazed. Winning first place made me realize just how far I'd really come. It was great knowing that all of the training, falls, and frustration of learning new tricks had paid off.

Many of the reporters I talked to wanted me to explain how I managed to get to the top of my sport in such a short time. They called me a natural and gave me the nickname "Little Ripper." I'm pretty shy, so talking about this in front of cameras and microphones was difficult. I did my best to make it clear that I owed my success to my coach Darin, who's one of the top wakeboarders in the world.

Darin is a five-time professional tour champ, and in the early 1990s, he invented more than half of the tricks done in wakeboarding. (Wakeboarding hasn't been around very long—an early version of the sport began in 1985. The World Wakeboarding Association, the governing body for the sport, was founded in 1990, which is when wakeboarding really started to become popular.)

Darin has a private lake not far from where I live, and I started taking lessons with him in September 1996. I was nervous the first few times I practiced with him, but then I really got into it. The more tricks I learned, the more I wanted to ride.

Darin thought I had great potential from the very beginning, and he told my mother I should get on the water as often as possible. Darin and I have been working together ever since.

He also talked to the people at his board company, Hyperlite, and now they sponsor me, helping to finance my training. In exchange, I use Hyperlite equipment when I compete.

At the X Games, Hyperlite supported me, as well as all of their other athletes. I have a total of eight sponsors now, including Hyperlite (which supplies my boards, boots, and rope), Vans (surf and street shoes), Hang Ten (clothing), Jetpilot (I wear their wetsuits), Mastercraft (they manufacture boats), Oakley (cool sunglasses), Freestyle (water-resistant watches), and Gravity Longboards (for skateboards).

Even though I love wakeboarding so much, it can be a difficult sport. It's easy to get tired from training so hard and traveling to tournaments (sometimes every weekend). Plus, wakeboarding can be dangerous, and some of my falls have hurt pretty bad.

The worst wipeout I've ever experienced happened while I was trying a new trick called a *scarecrow* (it's kind of like a somersault with a 180 degree turn in it). As I went into my rotation, my right knee hit the left side of my chin and banged into my

How I got started:

I grew up in a neighborhood of mostly boys, and I did everything they did. When they started wakeboarding, it was only natural for me to do it, too. I was 14 the first time I gave it a try. When I started wakeboarding, I was the only girl rider in the group, but I never let that stop me.

Accomplishments:

At the end of the 1997 season, I had been named Pro Tour Champion, X Games Gold Medalist, and World Champion, plus I set a world record for most points earned by a woman on the pro tour. In 1998, I won the bronze medal in the X Games and earned the titles of Pro Tour Champion and World Champion again.

How I stay motivated:

I fell in love with this sport from the moment I started, and this is my biggest motivation. Competing boosts my confidence whether I win or lose, and I love the positive feelings that result from a good performance.

My future:

My desire to compete is really strong, but I try not to set huge goals for myself. I prefer to take smaller steps, concentrating on one tournament at a time. My goals in school are reasonable, too—to stay at a 3.0 grade point average or higher. After I finish high school, I plan to go to college, but I have no idea what I'll major in.

teeth. I was knocked out. With my head underwater and blood streaming from my busted lip, I was in danger of drowning. Fortunately, Darin reacted quickly. He and a friend jumped in the water, clothes and all, and pulled me out.

They laid me on the platform of the boat, where I started breathing and coughing up water. I ended up going to the hospital, where I had a CAT scan, X-rays, and more than twenty stitches in my mouth and on my chin. Although I wasn't afraid to get back on my board, it took about four months before I had the nerve to try the same trick again.

Wakeboarding is a risky sport, but I believe in having the guts to go for what you want. If you let fear rule your world, you miss out on a lot of fun stuff.

How do you get beyond your fears? It helps to believe in yourself. Sometimes the only thing holding you back is *you.* Instead of saying that you *can't* do something, say "I *can* do it!" and find a way to prove yourself right. This positive approach helps me, and it can help you, too.

One of the most important things for any girl to remember is this: Don't be a follower. In other words, don't just do things because your friends (or boyfriend) do. What activity inspires you? Once you know, go for it and give it everything you've got!

Go Exploring

Launch Wakeboard Magazine
P.O. Box 500
Missouri City, TX 77459
1-800-310-7047
Launch Wakeboard includes athlete interviews, cool photos, special features, and cutting-edge info about the sport.

Wakeboarding 101
http://www.aub.mindspring.com/~alanhurd/
This Web site offers the lowdown on wakeboarding terminology, tips on technique, and information about getting started. You'll also find pictures, links to other wakeboarding sites, and information on schools and camps.

WakeWorld's Wakeboarding Web Site
http://www.wakeworld.com/
Online tournament info, links to riders, and news from the world of wake-boarding can all be found here. WakeWorld also has an email list, so you can exchange tips and hear from other wakeboarders.

Waterski.com
http://www.waterski.com
This is a great source for anyone who wants waterskiing-related informa-tion. Log on to find out about waterskiing, boating, and wakeboarding, and get the scoop on upcoming events.

Rachel Cook

------- *Teen* Athlete of the Year -------

Birthdate: 11/8/83
Hometown: Garland, Texas
School: St. Pius X School
Family: mom, Jean; dad, Kelly; sister, Juli (28)
Hobbies: basketball, track and field, softball, cheerleading, modeling, student ambassador

n April 1997, I was flipping through the pages of *Teen* magazine when a contest ad caught my eye: "Could you be the 1998 *Teen* Athlete of the Year?"

To enter the contest, you had to send a postcard listing your name, address, birthdate, age, grade point average, school, and grade level, plus the sports you participate in (including position, league, club, or school), awards you've won or records you've set, and leadership positions you've held. Right away, I got excited. Sports have always been a big part of my life. I'm a dancer, cheerleader, gymnast, ice skater, and softball player, but I love basketball and track and field the most. I decided to enter the contest.

My mom helped me put together a typed résumé to include with my entry. The résumé listed my school activities, my scholastic achievements, and my experiences in basketball, softball, and track and field. I described how I started playing basketball for a city league when I was in fourth grade, and over the next few years, continued finding other teams to play on until I was playing on a total of five different teams in 1996.

"To achieve success you've got to really want it."

— Rachel

I also told *Teen* about how I run track and compete in the high jump. In 1996, I broke my school's record in the high jump and 100 meter hurdles, and I set a league record in the 300 meter hurdles. That same year, I was named Female Track Athlete of the City Meet and Female Athlete of the Year at the City Meet for the Dallas Parochial League—the first time a sixth grader had won both awards.

My experience with the Texas Stars Track Club is something I'm really proud of, so I wrote about that, too. As a member of the track club, I won a silver medal for the state in the high jump in 1996, which earned me a spot on the Junior Olympic Team (where I placed thirteenth). In 1997, I made it to the state finals again and won the gold medal, as well as the Texas State Junior title with a high jump of 5 feet, 2 inches.

My basketball coach wrote a letter of recommendation for me, which I included with my other contest materials. I mailed the entire package to *Teen* and waited to see what would happen.

Four months later, I received a notice from the magazine telling me I was a semifinalist. I was surprised to hear that out of the 10,000 athletes who entered, I was one of the 48 chosen for the finals.

The letter came with a list of five questions for me to answer:

1. What do I think is the importance of athletics to teenagers?
2. What influence has athletics had on my life?
3. What has been my most important goal?
4. Where do I see myself in ten years?
5. What makes me feel extraordinary and deserving to be the 1998 Athlete of the Year?

Answering these questions allowed me to express how I feel about sports. I told the judges that my involvement in so many different sports has given me the chance to learn about myself and what I can handle. Sports have taught me to face challenges with determination and grace. And my involvement in sports has made me strive for my best, both on and off the field.

Because I'm an athlete, I've learned how to stay focused. This helps me at school because I get more out of my classes (which beats filling up a notebook with doodles). I've come to understand the value of teamwork and self-reliance, and how to balance the two. I've also discovered the importance of having a positive attitude, even when things aren't going my way.

At one time, I was too timid to try new things. Being an athlete has made me more open to new possibilities. For example,

I'm a member of the People to People Student Ambassador program through my school. This program was organized by former president Dwight D. Eisenhower to promote international friendship, and our group will be traveling to England, Ireland, and Scotland to learn firsthand about other cultures. If it weren't for my involvement in sports, I wouldn't have the courage to travel so far from home or the self-assurance to meet new people. Because I've played on so many different teams, making new friends isn't scary anymore (in fact, it's fun!).

How I got started:

I've been on the same softball team since I was six. When I first started playing softball, I wanted to play third base, but somebody else got that spot: LeAnn Rimes (yes, the singer . . . she's from Garland, too!). I ended up being the left fielder. I started playing basketball when I was ten, and I've been playing ever since. I play for an AAU (Amateur Athletic Union) team, as well as my school team. These athletic experiences fueled my interest in winning the *Teen* Athlete of the Year Award.

Accomplishments:

I took first place overall and won five gold medals (one in each event entered) in the 1998 City Track Meet. I'm also a student ambassador with the People to People program, a member of the Bishop Lynch Catholic High School basketball team (the top team in the country), and an honor student.

How I stay motivated:

My coaches have always told me that I'm a really good jumper and runner. Hearing this makes me feel good and motivates me to keep practicing, even on hot summer days. My parents and coaches encourage me without pushing, and I keep playing because it's what I like to do.

My future:

As *Teen* Athlete of the Year, I received a $5,000 college scholarship. I'm thinking of going to Stanford University in California to study medical science. No matter what I decide to do, I'll continue setting new goals for myself because I love how it feels to accomplish them.

Many young people feel like they don't fit in or belong (I've felt this way myself). Athletics give kids and teens a way to get involved and be part of a group. I believe that sports are the best way to find your place and discover your strengths. I told the contest judges that I think athletics provide a way for girls like me to stay healthy, both physically and emotionally. Sports have always done this for me.

I explained that my goals for the future are definitely centered around school and sports. I want to participate in track and field and play basketball in high school—maybe even become an All-American (an honor that shows you've reached the elite level of your chosen sport). Someday I'd love to win an Olympic gold medal in basketball or the high jump. In my heart, I believe that I have the strength and motivation to do it.

Once again, I put my entry in an envelope and sent it off. Then I waited . . . .

Rachel performs the high jump at the 1996 National Junior Olympics.

Four months later, guess what happened? I received word that I was one of the final sixteen contestants! I couldn't believe I'd made it so far. I knew I'd accomplished a lot as an athlete, but somehow I was still skeptical about winning. At that point, though, I started to get excited. What if I really *did* win?

I waited and waited to hear if I'd won. Right before Thanksgiving, a Federal Express package arrived for me. When I tore it open, I was stunned. The letter said, "Congratulations, you are the new 1998 *Teen* Athlete of the Year!"

The rest of the letter explained what I'd won and what I needed to do to collect the prizes. I could hardly absorb what

I was reading. I felt numb, amazed, completely overwhelmed. I kept saying, "I can't believe I won." Finally, after saying it enough times, I started shouting, "Yeah, I really won!" It was the best Thanksgiving ever.

As *Teen* Athlete of the Year, I was flown to Los Angeles for a photo shoot. My parents and I stayed at the Hotel Nikko in Beverly Hills. On the day of the shoot, we went to the University of California at Los Angeles (UCLA) to meet the people from *Teen* at the Drake Stadium track.

Everyone I met was so nice; they treated me like a queen! Michelle Sullivan, who set up the shoot, was great. She took extra time to make sure that everything was just right.

The production people chose what I would wear for the photo shoot, and then we got to work. They asked me to do athletic stretches on the track, while the photographers snapped pictures. Because I've done quite a bit of modeling, I was comfortable in front of the camera. I thought the photo shoot was a lot of fun.

My family and I spent the next three days seeing the sights in Los Angeles. We went to Disneyland, the House of Blues, and Rodeo Drive. We had such a good time together.

When the April 1998 issue of *Teen* appeared on the newsstands, I was so excited. Inside was a story about me, complete with photos. The article featured my background information, along with quotes about how I stay in shape, what I think of competition, how it feels to be part of a team, and what a great role model my mom is. At first, it was strange to see myself on the pages of a national magazine, but it was exciting, too.

Since then, I've continued playing sports, and I know I always will because I enjoy athletics so much. The feeling I get from sports is so great that I really can't put it into words. This positive feeling encourages me to keep setting goals and trying to reach them.

To do my best, I picture that one person who's a little faster than me, or has a better shot, or is able to sprint harder in the final moments of a race or game: I keep trying to be that person.

Go Exploring

A Kind of Grace by Jackie Joyner-Kersee (New York: Warner Books, 1997). This autobiography of the woman known throughout the world as the best female athlete ever is both honest and inspiring. She shares her personal struggles, including battling asthma and sports-related injuries, and describes how she rose above them to succeed.

JUMP Magazine
P.O. Box 55954
Boulder, CO 80322-5954
1-888-369-JUMP (1-888-369-5867)
JUMP, a magazine for girls, is all about fitness and feeling good. The articles cover topics like sports, nutrition, health, self-esteem, and more.

Teen Magazine
P.O. Box 52795
Boulder, CO 80322-2795
http://www.teenmag.com
Filled with fun and informative articles, *Teen* gives you the lowdown on fitness trends, celebrities, fashion, and more. Check out the magazine to find out about the *Teen* Athlete of the Year contest.

Cristen Powell
----------------- Drag Racer -----------------

Birthdate: 3/22/79
Hometown: Lake Oswego, Oregon
School: Linfield College
Family: dad, Casey; sisters,
Carrie (23) and Courtney (21)
Hobbies: No time for any!

People typically think of auto racing as a guy thing, but the truth is a lot of women race—and I'm one of them. I love the sensation of going down the dragstrip at speeds so fast the vibrations shake my entire body.

You know when you accelerate from a traffic light, and you can feel the force pushing you back in the seat? Well, the *dragster* (race car) feels ten times as powerful as that, and the acceleration doesn't stop until the race is over. This feeling is the biggest rush you can imagine, and it lasts the whole way down the quarter-mile length of the track.

The greatest day of my racing career was when my team won the Mopar Parts Nationals in Englishtown, New Jersey, on May 18, 1997. I was only eighteen. I skipped my high school prom so I could participate in the race, but it was worth it. My team had worked really hard all year for what we achieved that day.

"No one wins them all, but this shouldn't keep you from trying."

– Cristen

We knew that the competition would be intense. We'd be racing against Kenny Bernstein, who at the time was the world champion; Cory McClenathan, who was on the verge of a six-race winning streak; Gary Scelzi, the current points leader; and Bruce Sarver, a newcomer to the final round, like me.

Englishtown is like many of the other racetracks nationwide. After the quarter mile, there's a half mile or so of "shutdown area," where you slow your car down after the race. There are grand-stands almost all of the way down the racetrack. The cars roll underneath the tower (where the announcers and sponsors are) to the starting line, and when you look up all you can see is a mass of people.

I race in a Top Fuel Dragster, a cigar-shaped car that accelerates faster than any machine in the world, going from 0 to 100 miles per hour in less than a second. These cars have a 6,000 horsepower engine (about thirty-five times more powerful than an engine in a regular car), which is located behind the driver.

Although a drag race lasts less than five seconds, preparing the car for a run takes a lot of time, and the crew is a crucial part of the process. When I win a race, it isn't just me who wins; everybody on the team wins, too. Drag racing is a team sport, and we're all trying to accomplish the same thing—the win. There's nothing like flying across the finish line and feeling the thrill of victory.

Before the race begins, the crew has an hour and a half to completely strip the engine down to bare block (in other words, take it all apart to see which parts might need to be replaced), put it together, and fire it up again. About an hour before the run, we warm up the car to get heat in the motor, which allows us to simulate what will happen on the starting line when I slam down the throttle, also known as "flooring it."

I've never had a major accident, but safety is a huge concern in my sport. I exercise to stay in peak condition because in a crash I have a better chance of survival if my body is strong. Being in shape also means I "cut better lights" (have better reaction times) on the track.

The racing suit I wear reflects the dangers involved in my sport. My one-piece "firesuit" made of a special material called Nomex is three layers thick, which protects me by making it harder for fire to reach my skin. I also have to wear fireproof long underwear, socks, and shoes. I walk around in my gear for about a half hour before the race. The firesuit is hot, but after a few minutes I get used to it. My sweat helps cool me down.

Before I get into the dragster, I put in my earplugs, which attach to the two-way radio I use to talk to my crew. Believe me, once the race starts, I'm thankful to have my ears plugged—it's remarkably loud on the track. Unfortunately, the earplugs also block out the roar of the crowd, so I don't get to hear the applause after a win or a great run. The rest of the team gets to enjoy that . . . but I wouldn't give up *my* seat for the world.

Next, I put on my helmet and a pair of gloves that I wear under the firesuit. Before I zip up my firesuit, I tuck in my purple platypus Beanie Baby, a stuffed animal I got for my eighteenth birthday, who always rides with me. I also wear a neck collar and chin strap, which help prevent my head from being snapped back when the car roars off from the starting line.

When I'm all suited up, I walk to the back of the dragster to make sure the parachutes are ready to "pop" when I need them to. Because the dragster travels at such high speeds, I can't rely on just mechanical brakes to bring the car to a safe stop. This is where the chutes come in: As they fill with air, they help slow the car and bring it to a gradual halt.

Finally, I walk to the left side of the vehicle, swing my right leg over, and slide into my seat. Ed Tyler, one of my teammates, straps me into the car with my five-point safety harness (a racer's seat belt), and I'm set to go.

Once we fire up the car on the starting line, we do what's called a *burnout*—rolling the car through water and slamming the throttle down to spin the tires. The burnout removes rocks and dirt from the tires, lays down a patch of rubber on the track, and heats up both the motor and the tires for the run.

After the burnout, I back up the car to the starting line, and the crew performs a last-minute check. Then I roll up to "prestage," where a light goes on

Cristen gets ready to roll.

to signal that both cars are ready. Next, I turn the fuel pump on all the way to 100 pounds of pressure (using a lever in the cockpit), ease my foot off the clutch, and roll to the stage light. Now the race is about to happen!

At the Mopar Parts Nationals, my goal at the starting line was to clear my head. Because I'd been down the quarter-mile track many times before, I didn't need to think through every move; my body knew what to do. Drag racing is all about reactions— to the start, to handling the car, and to pulling the chutes.

I tried to keep calm, even though my heart was pounding. I watched the two small lights at the top of the "Christmas Tree," a set of lights used to start the race. At the flip of a switch, three larger amber lights appeared at the same time: As soon as the lights hit my eye, I put the pedal to the metal and let go of the brake. I was off!

The second the car started moving, 5 g's of force pushed against me. My arms were stretched out holding onto the steering wheel, and my face felt like it was being pulled tight by two hands.

Nothing I've ever experienced compares to a ride in a Top Fuel Dragster. It's what I can only imagine a ride in a space shuttle must feel like (and maybe even better).

The car traveled the first 60 feet in about eight-tenths of a second, and by that time, I was going about 100 miles per hour. The front wheels of the car were off the ground for the first 100 feet. By the end of the race, the car was going more than 300 miles per hour, and the whole way down the quarter mile, I clenched my teeth and waited for the right time to hit the parachutes.

On the final pass at the Mopar Parts Nationals, my engine blew up, so I didn't even think about who had won until I was safely out of the car. Many of the people who were watching the race thought I jumped out so quickly because I was excited about winning—but I did it because I thought I was on fire.

Looking back, I'm still amazed about that race. I was so proud of my team, and of course, the win. That day, I became the youngest woman, the second youngest person, and the fifth

How I got started:

For my sixteenth birthday, my dad gave me a trip to Frank Hawley's Drag Racing School because he knew I was interested in racing. I got "seat time," or behind-the-wheel practice during this three-day course. At the end of the course, I got my license to race—before I even had my regular driver's license (I earned *that* the day after camp was over).

Accomplishments:

So far, winning the Mopar Parts Nationals is my biggest accomplishment to date. But I'd earned six track records in 1996 before making the jump to Top Fuel. I broke the 300 mph mark 10 times, including a top speed of 307.27 mph. At the 1998 Northwest Nationals in Seattle, Washington, I broke the track record with an elapsed time of 4.59 seconds to earn the #1 qualifying spot (this also made me the quickest woman in the world!).

How I stay motivated:

I've always been driven to succeed, and I love to try new experiences. This positive attitude has helped me both on and off the track.

My future:

My next big goal in racing is to win the World Championship in Top Fuel. When it comes down to it, this is every racer's dream. College is another challenge in my life; I'm majoring in psychology at Linfield College in McMinnville, Oregon. I try to approach my studies with the same determination I have when I race.

woman in the history of the sport to win a national event in Top Fuel. All in all, that day was one of the best of my life.

As exhilarating as each race may be, I sometimes get intimidated or scared out on the track. When this happens, I tell myself to stay cool and focused. In the past, it was difficult for me to compete against the pros while I was still learning how to drive my car and get comfortable racing, but I overcame this challenge.

Still, even now, some veteran racers try to make me feel like I don't belong on the track. But I won't let myself get discouraged. Instead, I keep reminding myself why I race—because I LOVE this sport.

To me, drag racing is more than just the sport I compete in and the job I was hired to do—it's who I am. I want to be the best in the sport, but I know this won't happen overnight. At a young age, I was taught that I can do anything I set my mind to, and I'm willing to struggle and work hard for my achievements.

I'm challenged by being a young female athlete involved in a sport dominated by adult males. When people ask me if I want to be the fastest woman on the track, I say, "No, I want to be the fastest *person* on the track." They ask me if I think this is possible, and I assure them it is.

Go Exploring

Frank Hawley's Drag Racing School
P.O. Box 484
La Verne, CA 91750-0484
1-888-901-7223
http://www.frankhawley.com
Thrill-seekers who are at least 16 years old and have a valid driver's license can enjoy a one-time adventure driving a dragster or stock car. For those interested in more comprehensive experiences, longer training courses are available as well.

National Hot Rod Association (NHRA)
2035 Financial Way
Glendora, CA 91741
(626) 914-4761
http://www.nhraonline.com
The NHRA promotes interest in building and racing autos and motorcycles. Their Youth and Education Services program is devoted to educational activities for students, trackside and on school campuses. The Junior Drag Racing League is open to young people ages 8–17 who race half-scale dragsters powered by 5 horsepower engines.

Diana Silbergeld

------------- World Traveler -------------

Birthdate: 9/22/79
Hometown: Santa Monica, California
School: Wesleyan University
Family: mom, Carol; dad, Arthur; sister, Julia (14)
Hobbies: travel, hiking, singing, guitar, piano, cello, creative writing, painting, scuba diving, community service (feeding homeless people)

W hen I was five, my parents bought me a globe that lit up; it had bumps and ridges indicating the mountains and valleys. Running my hands over it, I had no idea that, one day, those small plastic continents would come to life for me.

My parents encouraged me to be a traveler. When my family traveled, our destination was never a place found in a glossy brochure. Instead, my parents wanted to show me the real world and to instill in me a sense of responsibility for leaving the earth a better place than I found it.

By the age of twelve, I had visited sixteen countries, slept in hotels with dirt floors and roaming chickens, been awakened by vultures attacking garbage cans, and tasted frog legs, yak-butter tea, and even dog. By fourteen, I had witnessed firsthand the Zapatista revolution in Chiapas, Mexico, lived on a sheep farm in New Zealand, and heard monkeys howl in Costa Rica.

When I was fifteen, I began spending my summers traveling with peer groups, facing physical and emotional challenges most people only imagine. At times, I felt as if I had fallen off a map, landing somewhere between the world of *Indiana Jones* and *The English Patient,* a scarf draped around my face to avoid desert dust.

In 1996, after spending four summers at an all-girls sleep-away camp, I decided that I wanted to spend my next few summers traveling. With the support and encouragement of my parents, I chose "Project Thailand" with a company called Global Routes. This program emphasized living with Thai families, traveling throughout Thailand, and getting involved in community service. I was fifteen and went abroad with nine students from all over the United States. The purpose of our journey was to plant trees, build a school addition, and teach English to young students.

On my first day of work in the remote village, I found myself standing alone in front of forty bright little Thai faces. My task was to teach English for two hours. After failing to get my students to comprehend the phrase "How old are you?" I didn't know what to do. Out of desperation, I pointed to the desk and said, "desk." I motioned for them to repeat what I'd said, and the forty children repeated "des" in unison. It was a start.

We made progress as I continued to teach the children the names of other objects in the room and words that described feelings. When the lesson ended and it was time for me to leave, a few students came up to me, handed me roses, and said, "We are sad," a phrase I had taught them.

In addition to teaching, I worked for six hours each day in the scorching sun, stacking cinder blocks, making cement from scratch, laying a concrete floor, and painting what would become a lunch area for the schoolchildren, plus other tasks. Despite the heat and hard work, I was energized by the friendly Thai people who had opened their homes and shared their lives with our group.

"Grab opportunities to try something new and stay determined in pursuing your goals."
– Diana

The beautiful children surrounded us as we worked, and I wondered what they thought of the situation. They probably found it strange that a bunch of "well-to-do" Americans had come halfway around the world to get sweaty and dirty building a school in this small village. Still, I knew that our work reached into the hearts of the people we were helping, making this experience more productive and rewarding for me than anything I'd ever done before.

The project taught me to care deeply about the needs of others, and when I returned home, I wanted to continue doing community service. I began to work at a local homeless shelter, picking up, delivering, and serving food, and I still work there regularly now. As a result of my experience in Thailand, community service became very important to me, and it gave me further inspiration to travel, work, and learn.

Last summer, I had the opportunity to explore another incredible part of the world. I spent six weeks in Tibet and Nepal with "Where There Be Dragons," an intense educational travel program. I made the trip with three group leaders who were fluent in the Tibetan and Nepali languages, as well as thirteen other American students.

This trip was the most daring adventure I've ever embarked on. My friends at home couldn't believe how far I was going or that I wanted to hike for days, eat strange foods, and be unable to take a shower. I threw myself into an uncomfortable situation that proved to be one of the most satisfying challenges I've ever faced.

I couldn't have prepared myself for the culture shock I experienced as I stepped off the plane in Kathmandu, Nepal. I walked across trash-covered streets, where barefoot children ran up to me, begging for money. We spent our first week in the country getting oriented to the different ethnic groups of the Himalayas and learning about the ancient history and traditions of the Tibetan culture.

We also learned about the realities of twentieth-century political oppression. I became aware that there were more Chinese people living in Tibet than Tibetans. The Chinese government took over Tibet in 1949, forcing many people to flee in search of freedom. Even the Dalai Lama, the political and spiritual leader of Tibet, lives in exile in northern India.

Many Tibetans fled to Nepal, and they live there as refugees, without many of the basic rights that most people take for granted. They can't travel or even consider returning to their homelands. They can't vote or buy land. Yet, the Tibetans in exile were the most dignified and hopeful people I've ever met.

My traveling group lived among host families in a Tibetan community in Nepal. The family I stayed with seemed content with their way of life. The parents and their four children occupied a tiny two-room dwelling and shared an outdoor shower and outhouse with five other families. This family had no phone, car, refrigerator, or washing machine. There was little variation in their daily lives: They worked, cooked, cleaned, and prayed. Maybe they seemed happy with their simple lifestyle because they had no idea of what they lacked. They were determined to preserve their culture and the ability to speak their own language freely, and they seemed filled with certainty that they would someday return home to Tibet.

Diana is surrounded by a group of children in Baktapur, Nepal.

From Kathmandu, we trekked to Mount Kailash in western Tibet. According to Buddhists and Hindus, Mt. Kailash, the source of four major rivers (including the Ganges), is the holiest mountain on earth. Every year, hundreds of people make long pilgrimages to this sacred spot—some walking for months from India, most falling down to weep and pray when they finally see it.

Our twenty-seven-day trek began in old Land Cruisers, driving for six days across a desert with no roads. The climate in Tibet is harsh; there's little rainfall or vegetation, and it's very cold during the winter. Although the "Land of the Snows," as it's called, is barren, it was one of the most beautiful landscapes I've ever seen. Even now, I can vividly recall the yellow hills reaching up to a blinding blue sky.

When we arrived at Mt. Kailash, I could feel the mystery and power the mountain held. This monumental, narrow, snow-covered peak sits in the middle of a flat, parched desert. It's customary for Tibetan Buddhists to walk clockwise around a holy site like a monastery or *stupa* (a sacred monument to Buddha), and they believe that walking around Mt. Kailash rids one of a lifetime of sin. Our group embarked on its own four-day circumambulation around the holy mountain, hiking up the steep passes, carrying all of our gear on our backs.

When we reached the highest pass at 18,600 feet, we shared our trail mix with Tibetan pilgrims who, upon finishing the climb, sang out with joy and threw bundles of papers into the air. The papers had prayers written on them, and they were tossed into the air to be carried to heaven.

How I got started:

My interest in traveling the world has developed from an inherent need to wonder and learn.

Accomplishments:

I traveled to Thailand with Global Routes and completed "Alpine Challenge" (hiking across the Swiss and French Alps) with Overland Travel. I was recognized for outstanding community service work (with homeless shelters) at Harvard-Westlake High School. I was also a member of the Harvard-Westlake Chamber Singers.

How I stay motivated:

The people I've met while traveling, and who share my same excitement and interests, are what motivate me. I also feel inspired by community service.

My future:

At Wesleyan University, I plan to major in Asian studies or Spanish. I'd like to spend a year abroad in Asia or Latin America while I'm in college. I know that no matter what career I choose, travel will be a part of it.

On that small, rocky peak, I felt like I was on top of the world. I saw colorful Tibetan prayer flags—multicolored squares of cloth, tied in a chain and placed on mountaintops by people who believe that when the wind blows, their prayers will go to heaven. The beautiful flags whipped and waved against the cloudless, azure sky.

On our trip down the mountain, I thought about how I hadn't showered for almost a month. I also thought about the nomad families I'd seen in Tibet, who probably didn't even know what a television set was. My mind drifted home to my own fluffy towels, toilet, and perfumed soaps. "These people have no idea how I really live!" I thought; they only knew that I was a "rich" American. When they offered me yak-butter tea in exchange for a few words, it occurred to me that these people were rich, too, in their simplicity, generosity, and spiritual devotion.

While hiking back from Mt. Kailash, I had the opportunity to visit a "sky burial ground." On the Tibetan plateau, there are no trees, and three-quarters of the year, the soil is solid ice, making cremations and burial impossible. When someone dies there, the body is taken to a sacred place on a hill and a "sky burial" is given. The corpse is chopped up into small pieces, and the bones and hair are removed. Vultures and birds gather to eat the remaining body. Tibetans believe that, in this way, the dead are carried up into the heavens, and the soul stays behind to be reborn.

I crawled out of my tent before sunrise on a crisp July morning. Approaching the burial ground, I stepped over the last knoll and steeled myself to see something disturbing. Nausea swept over me as my boots crunched over countless pieces of clothing, shoes, clumps of hair, and bones from the dead. All was silent as the sun appeared over the ridge.

I held my breath and entered the main ceremonial area. I couldn't see the ground within the circle of stones, for it was covered by clothing—some belonging to adults and some to babies, and most of it bloody. Next to the site, an ax lay on a rock. A bird called in the distance. I headed back to my tent, having been slapped in the face by death.

As I hiked through the quiet valley, I wasn't shocked or disgusted by the details of what I'd just witnessed. Instead, I was angry—angry that I didn't feel the comfort of these spiritual beliefs and that my parents hadn't taught me something so beautiful to believe in. In my own culture, death had always been hidden, denied, whispered about. I wasn't supposed to see it; death wasn't supposed to be part of life. I became annoyed about how I'd been raised, and I wondered what I would one day teach my own children about death and spirituality.

Immersed in Tibetan culture, I learned about the life of Buddha, reincarnation, meditation, and chanting, as well as the belief that all life is precious and desire causes suffering. I began to think seriously about my own culture and upbringing, and how everyone I know is always striving for something better—higher grades, better health, more money, nicer clothes, a fancier car. I wondered if I stopped aiming for some unattainable perfection, would I be happy to the core? These new ideas compelled me to question my ethics and deeply rooted beliefs. Traveling forced me to reexamine all that I knew.

One afternoon, on our hike back into Nepal, we stopped to set up tents for the night. I was hungry, so two guys from the group came with me to look for a villager who could sell us some food. The village, like most in Nepal, consisted of about five houses with small plots of land around them for growing crops. The three of us walked up to a house and asked a woman (in Tibetan) if she had any food to sell. She nodded and motioned for us to follow her up a wooden ramp to her house. Buffalo lived underneath the house to keep it warm during the winter, as well as to provide milk and meat.

The woman led us into her home. The floor and walls were made of mud, and the windows were holes covered with plastic bags. In the middle of the room was a small pit that served as the stove. She knelt and began boiling water to make potatoes for us. We took off our boots and sat cross-legged across from her. Her three children entered the room and stared at us, wide-eyed. The younger ones probably had never seen a white person before. The family's clothes were filthy and, most likely, were the only ones they owned.

As the woman cooked, I stared curiously at her. She was strong (and had to be to live her harsh life). Her hair was a rich black color, and her skin was tough and weathered. She stirred the water, blew on the fire, and fixed her child's hair with grace, and it appeared as if she could do all of these things with her eyes closed. The woman smiled and glanced over at me as she tended the potatoes, seeming to understand what I was thinking. We stared at each other for a moment, in awe, trying to conceive the difference between our lives.

Every day, I remind myself of moments when I was amazed by the differences between my culture and that of other people I've met. When I flash back to that afternoon in Nepal, where I ate boiled potatoes in the home of a stranger, my own life suddenly seems strange and inconceivable.

The deeper into a cultural experience I go, the purer I feel. Traveling to remote places gives me a sense of freedom. I don't have to worry about the complications and distractions of my life at home—what to wear, what I need to do, who I forgot to call. Instead, I live life at its most basic level—eating, sleeping, connecting with fellow human beings, and thinking about my place in the universe. I don't need nice hotels or clean laundry; what I *do* need is to learn, grow, and keep exploring other cultures and ways of life.

My journeys have taught me to be more content with what I have and to help others who are less fortunate. My goal is to improve the world in any way that I can. I can't be certain where this responsibility will take me—a doctor in a third world country, a teacher, a *National Geographic* journalist—but I'm looking forward to the journey.

Go Exploring

Seven Years in Tibet by Heinrich Harrer (New York: Putnam Publishing Group, 1997). This book recounts the true-life adventure of Austrian mountaineer Heinrich Harrer who, in 1939, set out to climb the highest peak in the Himalayas. After being captured by British soldiers and sent to a prisoner of war camp in northern India, he escaped to Lhasa, the spiritual center of Tibet. Here Heinrich befriended the young Dalai Lama and became his tutor for the next seven years. In 1997, a movie based on the book was released: Brad Pitt stars as Heinrich Harrer.

Where There Be Dragons
P.O. Box 4651
Boulder, CO 80306
1-800-982-9203
http://www.wheretherebedragons.com

This program offers challenging educational journeys to such destinations as China, Thailand, Mongolia, Vietnam, Nepal, Tibet, and India for students ages 15 and up. The travels include cultural immersion, homestays, and service projects.

Leslee Olson

Birthdate: 3/14/78
Hometown: Bend, Oregon
Family: mom, Kathy; dad, Gary;
brothers, Thor (15) and Ty (12)
Hobbies: working out, playing tennis,
surfing, skateboarding, biking, running,
hanging out with friends and family

Snowboarding gives me such an amazing feeling. You have so much freedom surfing on the snow—it's almost like you're floating.

No matter how many times I do it, going off a cliff always seems new and exciting. It's the most awesome feeling to spin upside down while airborne. When I'm in the air, I'm a little scared inside, but I just tell myself I can do it. Everything happens so fast: I take off, spin upside down, get lost in the air, and before I know it, I'm back on the ground. I love it, and for me, there's no better way to have fun.

When I started snowboarding as a young girl, I was practically the only female snowboarder at Mount Bachelor, the ski resort near my hometown. I hung out with guys who were snowboarders. Because they were better at the sport than I was, I pushed myself to work harder. At the time, there were no *halfpipes* (U-shaped channels carved in the snow for snowboarders to perform tricks and jumps) or snowboard parks for us to use—just lots of challenging terrain and powdery snow, courtesy of Mother Nature.

We were into *freeriding,* or making our way down the mountain without a set course, using obstacles like tree stumps and rocks to perform airborne stunts (or, in snowboarder lingo, to "catch air"). We'd carve fresh paths down the hill in search of new obstacles all the time. I had fun riding with all of my friends, and two years later, my skills had improved a lot. When I was eleven, I decided to give snowboard racing a try, and I discovered that it was more exciting than I had ever imagined.

When I graduated from high school, I faced a big decision: Should I try to make it as a professional snowboarder or go to college? I didn't know if I was good enough to go pro, but I had a dream of snowboarding professionally, and I wasn't ready to give it up. I chose to train and to race in as many competitions as I could. My persistence and determination paid off because now I'm on the pro tour.

I feel so lucky because I think I have the best career in the world. I get to travel and spend time with my best friends, doing what I love. Snowboarding events have taken me to Europe ten times, to Japan twice, and to various places throughout the United States and Canada. The traveling has been a great learning experience and has opened my eyes to different cultures. I love meeting new people, and I've made so many strong friendships because of snowboarding.

I've also had the chance to get involved in some wonderful events. On April 18, 1998, I took part in Boarding for Breast Cancer (BBC) at Sierra-at-Tahoe, a California ski resort. BBC is an annual event that combines snowboarding, music, and education to help increase awareness about breast cancer.

BBC began in 1996 in memory of Monica Steward, a clothing designer for a snowboarding apparel company, who lost her battle against breast cancer at age twenty-nine. Along with Kathleen Gasperini and Lisa Hudson, Monica came up with the concept of a "snowboard Lollapalooza" (a mix of snowboarding contests and alternative music) to raise awareness about the disease among young people. She died two months before the first BBC event took place.

"You have to ignore people who try to discourage you. Associate with positive people instead."
– Leslee

Boarding for Breast Cancer is now held as a celebration of life. The event raises money for the Breast Cancer Fund and the Susan G. Komen Foundation, which are nonprofit organizations dedicated to improving research, treatment, and early detection techniques, as well as educating the public about this devastating disease.

At BBC 1998, the festivities included halfpipe and "Big Air" demonstrations (when boarders go off a jump and do tricks that are judged for style and difficulty) by pro snowboarders, including me. There were also amateur boarding sessions, lectures by breast cancer survivors, and performances by big-name bands like the Foo Fighters, Moby, Royal Crown Revue, and Supersuckers. Over 4,000 people came to watch, and the ticket sales, raffles, donations, sponsors, and product sales helped raise more than $112,000.

I really enjoyed BBC because the event was for a good cause and also for fun. All of the snowboarders who appeared at BBC were there to enjoy themselves and to compete. However, we weren't under pressure like we were earlier that year when trying to make the Olympic team that would compete in Nagano, Japan. It was a relief to ride and perform simply for the thrill of it and for the benefit of the crowd.

For me, BBC stood as a symbol of how good my life is and how lucky I truly am. I was there with my best friends (pro boarders Tina Basich and Shannon Dunn), doing what I love to benefit a worthy cause. Not only did we get to compete and entertain the crowd, but we also got to hang out with the Foo Fighters. It was a beautiful, sunny California day, and I thought, "Does it get any better than this?"

At the event, the snowboarders started out riding the half-pipe, then watched the bands. After an autograph session and more snowboarding performances came the Big Air contest. The jump I was going to do was a hard one, but I told myself, "You can do it!" I stayed focused and decided to go for it 100 percent.

When it was my turn, I did a *rodeo flip* (an inverted aerial spin, also known as a 720). I kind of "sketched" on the landing, which means I bobbled a bit on the board and didn't land cleanly. But everyone cheered for me because of the difficulty of the trick. I enjoyed performing this big jump for all of the judges and spectators, and I ended up earning second place. After the prizes were awarded (I won a camera), we relaxed by listening to the bands play. The whole event was a blast from beginning to end.

It was also a learning experience. Watching the videos shown at BBC, and listening to the speakers, made me realize what a terrible disease breast cancer is. Being young doesn't necessarily make you immune to this form of cancer, and I learned that early detection is the key to surviving. When the breast cancer survivors spoke, I felt moved and inspired. I was proud to be part of such a meaningful event.

I don't have any regrets about the path I've chosen in my life. I followed my dreams and found happiness for myself. Unfortunately, some people have tried to dampen my enthusiasm by telling me that I should "just go to college." I know that college is important and, for many people, it's the best choice.

But for me, right now, being an athlete is the best choice. I've learned that to be an athlete, I have to be in control of my own destiny and believe in myself completely.

Attitude is everything. To make it in sports, especially at the professional level, the crucial ingredient is a positive attitude. No matter who you are or what you do, *you* have the power to choose your mood and outlook.

I choose to have a good outlook on life. My career as an athlete makes me happy, and I'm grateful for

Leslee "catches air" in Hintertux, Austria.

that. Although I sometimes get tired and stressed out from all of the traveling and constant racing, I tell myself to make the best of it. My positive attitude always pulls me through.

How I got started:

My uncle was a snowboarder, and the more I watched him "surf" the snow, the more interested I became. He offered to teach me, and before I knew it, we were boarding together every weekend. From the very first time I strapped my feet onto the snowboard at age nine, I loved the sport.

Accomplishments:

1998: Second place, U.S. Open Super G; Master of the Board Boardercross Champion. 1997: Junior World Big Air Champion; second place, FIS World Cup Halfpipe (Mt. St. Anne); second place, U.S. Open Banked Slalom; third place, FIS World Cup Halfpipe (Mt. Bachelor); second floor, ISF World Ranking. 1996: First place overall, Junior World Championship; second place, U.S. Open Super G; Junior Rider of the Year.

How I stay motivated:

The support of my teammates, coaches, sponsors, friends, and family helps keep me motivated. My goal is to keep getting better, for them and for me.

My future:

I hope to compete in Salt Lake City at the 2002 Olympics and come home with a medal in the giant slalom (a course that tests speed, strength, and tenacity). I also enjoy the thrill of doing tricks and stunts while airborne, so I plan to keep focusing on freestyle boarding.

I've had years of experience in this sport, but I still get scared or doubt my ability. Sometimes I have to face a racing course that's really icy, and I can't seem to "catch an edge" (this is when you dig the edge of the board into the snow to help control your speed, direction, and turns). Then my board scrapes over the rock-hard surface, and I feel like I can't get enough traction to carve a turn. Other times, I feel intimidated when I'm approaching a jump that seems too big. I always go for it anyway, and usually, I discover that it wasn't as hard as I thought. Believing in myself is the key.

No matter what the situation, I push away my doubts and urge myself to succeed. Deep down, I know that I have the desire, determination, and heart to face any challenge that comes my way.

Challenging myself regularly helps me improve my performance. I love competing and hearing everyone cheering and encouraging me. Their support makes me feel like I can do anything, and when I've done something to the best of my ability, I'm really satisfied. It gives me a huge feeling of accomplishment.

There's a saying that goes like this: "One of God's greatest miracles is to enable ordinary people to do extraordinary things." I believe in the wisdom of these words. You can accomplish anything you set your mind to, but only if you believe in yourself. You have to feel good about your talents and abilities, and you have to have a goal. Ask yourself what you really want; then zero in on your target and hang on to your dream until you've made it come true.

One of my friends wrote me a letter a long time ago, saying: "Reaching for dreams is never easy, for strength and courage are lonely friends. But those who reach for the stars walk in stardust." I've kept these words in my heart ever since.

Go Exploring

I Know Absolutely Nothing About Snowboarding by Steve Eubanks (Nashville: Rutledge Hill Press, 1997). This book introduces everything a beginner needs to know about snowboarding—from proper equipment and etiquette to a brief history and the language used on the slopes.

(Sick): A Cultural History of Snowboarding by Susanna Howe (New York: St. Martin's Press, 1998). This book offers a historical perspective on how the sport of snowboarding has helped shape pop culture.

Snowboarding to the Extreme! by Bill Gutman (New York: Tor Books, 1997). Learn about the sport of snowboarding, from the basics (like turning and stopping) to advanced moves (like racing, freestyle, and riding the halfpipe).

 Burton Snowboards
80 Industrial Parkway
Burlington, VT 05401
http://www.burton.com

This Web site offers advice on gear and how to choose the right snowboard, plus bios and interviews with top Burton snowboarders. Information is also available about Burton's after-school program, "Chill," which gives kids in cities a chance to learn how to snowboard (clothing, equipment, lessons, and transportation are all provided). Chill programs are available in Seattle, Washington; Boston, Massachusetts; and Burlington, Vermont, and they will soon be expanding to other cities. For more details, contact Burton at the above address.

Lisa Taylor-Parisi
------------ Circus Performer ------------

Birthdate: 3/4/83
Hometown: Essex Junction, Vermont
School: Berkshire School
Family: mom, Tobe; dad, Anthony; brothers, Christopher (25), Max (23), Timothy (21), Beau (21), and Matthew (8); sister, Elizabeth (24)
Hobbies: weight lifting, ballet, saxophone, track, pole vaulting, crew (rowing)

love the thrill of the tightrope. When I'm walking on the high wire, I feel different and strange (but in a good way). It's like I'm on the edge of life itself.

The high wire is only 6 feet above where I stand, which doesn't seem too intimidating when I have both feet planted securely on the ground. But as soon as I begin to climb the ladder to my platform, all I can think about is my body creeping higher and higher into the air . . . and far off the ground. When I reach the top and look down, my breath catches a little.

"You can accomplish any goal as long as you have a positive attitude."

– Lisa

Gazing downward, I see the circus floor far below. I have to adjust my body, mind, and feet to a completely different type of foothold. With just a wire between the ground and me, I always take my first step cautiously. It doesn't matter whether I've walked on a tightrope hundreds of times before: The first couple of steps always give me the jitters.

As I become more comfortable, I concentrate on my posture. Standing up straight looks more professional than walking hunched over.

Before each trick I perform on the wire, I think about the moves I'll make. I'm careful not to take my eyes off the end of the wire, and I focus my attention on this stable spot to help me keep my balance. It's scary to perform on a tightrope, and I worry about tripping or taking a bad step. In fact, I've fallen off the wire in performances, and when this happens, it's a challenge to keep smiling and continue the act. Over the years, I've come to realize that my fears help protect me. If I were to become too relaxed, I might make more mistakes.

My goal during every routine is to make each step flawless. I want the crowd to feel a sense of wonder and awe, and to be pleased with my performance. When I hear the audience applaud, I feel happy and proud.

I was nine years old when I went to Circus Smirkus Camp in a nearby town. This camp is run by the international Circus Smirkus, which is headquartered in Greensboro, Vermont. At the time, I was too young to join the actual Circus Smirkus troupe, but I had lots of fun learning a variety of circus skills, including juggling, clowning, tumbling, and swinging on the trapeze.

After a week of practice, we performed under the colorful circus tent. Friends and family came to watch, and even though I was a little nervous, I already knew from my ballet performances that I enjoyed being on stage.

The following year, I convinced my mom to let me try out to become a Circus Smirkus trouper, so I could work and travel with the circus for eight weeks during the summer. I didn't have any spectacular tricks planned for tryouts, but

Lisa performs on the tightwire with Circus Smirkus.

Rob Mermin, the director of the program, explained that he selected kids not for their special talents but for their enthusiasm, positive attitude, and willingness to work hard and try new things. Knowing this helped me relax.

At tryouts, we did all sorts of fun activities, like silly miming, and Rob encouraged us to really "get into it," which I did. Two weeks later, he called to ask me if I was ready to become a Circus Smirkus trouper for the 1993 summer tour. I said, "YES!"

Greensboro is pretty much in the middle of nowhere. Rob has an old, rambling farmhouse that serves as the troupe headquarters. Everyone arrived at the end of June, which marked the beginning of the circus season. The other performers were boys and girls from ages nine to nineteen, and they came from all over the world (the United States, Canada, Japan, Israel, England, Mongolia, Russia) to learn how to be circus troupers.

Most of us stayed in the barn, which has small cubicles resembling sleeping compartments on trains (I know it doesn't sound very glamorous—it wasn't!). There were four to eight bunk beds per compartment, and we had to cram all of our belongings into this small space. The crowded quarters helped us all get to know each other better.

During the first week of practice, troupers tested their skills in a variety of activities, with help from coaches and older troupers. Several of the coaches were from the Moscow Circus, which has the world's best circus training school. The practice sessions were designed to let everyone explore what they were interested in and good at.

My special interest was the tightrope. When I walked across the wire, I used a large fan for balance. (Holding onto a prop, like a pole or fan, helps tightrope artists maintain their center of gravity.) The girl who had been the tightrope walker in years past returned to Greensboro from her tour with Cirque du Soleil, a world-renowned circus founded in Québec in 1984. She coached me on the wire and even showed me how to make my own fan.

By the second week of Circus Smirkus, everyone had begun to develop individual acts, revolving around a particular theme. Soon the entire show began to take form.

Life as a circus trouper was a lot of fun—and a lot of work. Each morning at 8:45, all of the troupers met for warm-ups, followed by two hours of acrobatics. After a short break, we practiced juggling and ate lunch. Then we worked on our individual acts, selected costumes, and learned how to apply makeup. In the late afternoon, we had free time; sometimes we went to a nearby lake to swim or just relax.

Everyone was assigned chores. With so many people residing at the farmhouse, life could become messy and disorganized without a plan. The chores were a pain, but they were important and taught us teamwork. Troupers were expected to do everything from washing dishes to cleaning bathrooms (ugh!). Usually, we tried to get our work done right after breakfast, so we could move on to our acts.

In the evenings, we ate dinner together, then attended a council meeting. Here we discussed the good things that

How I got started:

When I was a little girl, my mother took me to see the Big Apple Circus in a nearby town. After watching the young girls perform on the elephants, I was so excited that I decided I wanted to be in a circus just like them. I've been traveling as a trouper with Circus Smirkus every summer since 1993.

Accomplishments:

1998: Second place, U.S. Weight Lifting Federation Junior Championship (53 kilo weight class); third place, New England Secondary School pole vaulting competition. 1997: Second place, U.S. Weight Lifting Federation Junior Championship (46 kilo weight class); second place, Team U.S.A. Competition (50 kilo weight class); coxswain for Berkshire School Girls Varsity Crew Team (our boat came in second place at the Head of the Connecticut, Secondary School Division).

How I stay motivated:

I love to practice and be on stage. Whether I'm on the tightrope or weight lifting, it makes me feel really good to do something I know I can do.

My future:

I'm young, and I still have plenty of time to decide what I want to do. I enjoy trying new activities at school, and I look forward to each new tour with the circus. I take life as it comes.

happened during the day, as well as any problems we were experiencing. The challenges of living and performing in the circus were good ones, but sometimes difficulties or frustrations occurred. The council meetings helped us deal with these problems.

For the remaining six weeks of the circus, we took our two-hour show on the road. The circus traveled the New England countryside in a big yellow and blue school bus, making stops in Massachusetts, New Hampshire, and Vermont.

Once the tour began, life got hectic, and things moved at a fast pace. We usually performed two shows a day, seven days a week, with an occasional day off. We put on shows at resort areas, daycare centers, museums, and libraries. Plus we gave workshops for local kids to learn basic circus tricks like juggling and acrobatics. We slept in sleeping bags at school dormitories, recreational centers, or in the homes of local people who invited us to stay with them. Being on the road was tiring but lots of fun.

While traveling, we still had to do chores. Our jobs included helping to set up the one-ring tent (which took at least seven hours), cleaning up in and around the tent, and organizing the costumes. The best job was working at the concession stand, making and selling popcorn, cotton candy, and snow cones.

During each show, I worked with a boy who was a tightrope walker like me. Our routine included quick dance steps in time to the music, hops, skips, 180 degree turns, 360 degree turns, small and fast jumps, big and slow jumps, and other tricks. We performed together and did individual moves. In one of our more daring feats, my partner lay down on the wire, and I walked over him; then I precariously lowered my body into a sitting position and waited as he jumped over me.

Our final performance was back in Greensboro. Our families, friends, and other supporters who attended the show proved to be our most enthusiastic audience. As we took our final bow, we all felt kind of sad that the circus season was over, but we were incredibly proud of how much we had learned and grown.

Whenever I perform, I feel really good inside, especially when the audience seems impressed. It's satisfying to work hard on a difficult trick and perform it well. My hope is to create magical moments to share with the crowd, and I love knowing that some of the girls and boys who watch my tightrope act may be inspired to become performers, too.

I'm a risk taker at heart. And when you're a risk taker, you're always facing new challenges and hurdles. I practice a lot and work hard to perfect my tricks, despite the risk of getting hurt. With each new trick I learn, there's always the chance of making a mistake. Sometimes the mistake occurs in front of a huge crowd, but to me, performing before a live audience—knowing that each person is watching in wonder—is worth the risk.

Positive thinking helps me overcome any discouragement I may face. If I make a mistake, perform a trick poorly, or fall, I don't let myself feel defeated. Instead, I concentrate on getting past the feeling of "I can't," so I can change it to "I can," and then to *"I did it!"*

Go Exploring

Circus Smirkus: A True Story of High Adventure and Low Comedy by Rob Mermin (Greensboro, VT: Circus Bar, 1997). With more than 150 photographs, this book tells the story of Circus Smirkus and how kids of all ages have fulfilled their dream of going off to join the circus. You'll find out what it's really like to live the daring and adventurous life of a circus performer.

Cirque du Soleil
http://www.cirquedusoleil.com
Cirque du Soleil is a blend of circus arts and street performance, wrapped up in spectacular costumes and fairyland sets, and staged to magical music and lighting. There are no animals in Cirque du Soleil productions—only sheer human energy. Check out their Web site for more information about their innovative circus and tour.

Circus Smirkus Headquarters
1 Circus Road
Greensboro, VT 05841
(802) 533-7125
http://www.greenmtns.com/circus

Circus Smirkus offers two-week summer camps for beginners (ages 8–14), as well as a touring youth circus.

Melissa Marshall

Birthdate: 1/22/76
Hometown: Harlem, New York
School: Barry University (graduate studies)
Family: mom, Brenda; dad, Willie, Sr.; brothers,
Curtis (34), Kelvin (30), Joseph (17), and
Willie, Jr. (13); sisters, Cindy (33), Wanda (29),
Natasha (17), and Tiasha (15)
Hobbies: desktop publishing, reading,
basketball, golf, tennis, community service,
volunteer emergency medical technician,
American Red Cross CPR and first aid instructor

G rowing up in the borough of Manhattan and the neighbor-hood of Harlem has had a profound effect on the person I am today. I was raised in a very supportive family, with lots of love and encouragement. Yet, I grew up with everyday scenes of drug addicts and dealers on street corners, and the disgusting filth of some of New York City's streets.

Despite these challenges, many people in my community served as positive role models for me. During my childhood and adolescent years, these positive examples (both adults and peers) helped combat the negative stereotypes prevalent in my community. These invaluable role models demonstrated another way—a better way—to live my life.

The love and support of others, including my parents, family, friends, and most importantly, God, have made me who I am today—a young African-American woman determined to make a difference in the world. Because of the support I've received, I've developed a burning desire to give back what has been given to me.

My parents always talked about the importance of receiving a quality education. In high school, I became very involved in academics and in the community. By the time I got to college, my desire to help others was like a fireball waiting to explode. I joined the Student Government Association's community service committee, hoping it would serve as a way for me to get involved, help others, and make a difference.

On a cold, windy Saturday morning in January, our group was taken to what appeared to be nothing more than a vacant lot. My first thought was, "What are we going to do *here?* This is just an old dirt-filled lot." On that abandoned scrap of land I was introduced to one of the greatest grassroots community-based organizations I've ever come to know: Habitat for Humanity.

Habitat for Humanity is a nonprofit organization founded in 1976 by Millard and Linda Fuller, millionaires who gave up the pursuit of money to help others become independent homeowners. The Fullers' mission was to eliminate poverty housing. Habitat for Humanity is comprised of Habitat International (the headquarters for the organization, located in Americus, Georgia), local affiliates, and campus chapters. Since the organization first began, it has built thousands of homes all over the world.

What I most admire about the organization is its strong work ethic, ideals, and principles. One of my favorite Habitat mottoes is: "Giving a hand up, not a handout." Habitat homeowners help build not only their own houses but also those of future homeowners, which creates a sense of community. Habitat helps people learn to help themselves, fostering more productive, active citizens. This leads to better homes, schools, and communities— and better lives.

Highly skilled and trained construction coordinators instruct the Habitat for Humanity volunteers. The volunteers learn how to do everything from pouring concrete and laying a foundation, to installing insulation, drywall (a type of plasterboard for walls), and carpet, to painting the homes inside and out.

"When you help others with a sincerity of heart, you're filled with a sense of purpose and accomplishment."

– Melissa

I was eager to do my part, and I soon learned that I wasn't the only one. Four other individuals helped me found the Students Raising Awareness campus chapter of Habitat for Humanity at Hampton University in Virginia.

We posted flyers, and we placed advertisements in the school's newspaper, on electronic bulletin boards, and on the radio. The response from the campus and community was overwhelming. Students, faculty members, and our affiliate,

Peninsula Habitat for Humanity, actively wanted to get involved and work together to eliminate poverty housing.

I can remember the very first time that our campus chapter ventured as a unit to work on a house. It was a windy autumn morning in early November. The sky was clear, and the sun was shining brightly. At 8 A.M. sharp, our chapter members met to carpool students to the Habitat for Humanity site.

As we traveled to the nearby site, I thought about what we were going to do that day. Many of us had never worked on a house before and were either nervous, overwhelmed with excitement, or just sleepy (after all, it was early for college students to be up on a Saturday morning!). I was just excited to be heading into the unknown.

When we arrived at our destination, I stared at a two-story home that appeared to be completed on the outside, except for the landscaping. The house was surrounded by deep brown soil.

I saw that the home was constructed of wood and had been painted a pretty baby-blue color. Workers had installed windows on the left side of the house; on the right side and the back of the house, clear plastic bags that covered the window frames were flapping in the breeze. A wooden post, about 8 feet high, was planted firmly in the yard. Neatly centered on the post was a white foam board with "Peninsula Habitat for Humanity" printed on it. Underneath were the names of local churches and schools that had helped build the home.

We entered the house. Standing inside was a petite Caucasian woman who appeared to be in her mid-thirties. She was dressed in tan workboots, tapered blue jeans, and a gray sweater. Her hair was shoulder length and dark. She held an electric saw in her left hand and a 4 foot slab of drywall in her right.

"Hello," she said brightly. "I'm Marie, and you all must be the crew from Hampton University."

I replied, "Hi! Do you know where I can find the construction coordinator?"

What she said next was something I didn't expect. "You're looking at her."

Here I was, a woman of the nineties who believed that a woman could do anything a man could do, but I had expected the construction coordinator to be male. What a pleasant surprise Marie was. Any gender stereotypes about construction workers were crushed by this powerful woman of 5 feet, 4 inches.

As I looked around the house, I wondered who it would belong to once it was finished. Just then, I saw an African-American woman with a smile that could light up the world. I understood right away that the home was going to be hers. A single mother with three children, the woman worked as a secretary during the day and took college classes in the evenings. She and her children welcomed us with open arms, offering us cookies and juice.

Melissa is hard at work on a Habitat house in Newport News, Virginia.

After we all introduced ourselves, we got to work. Our task and goal for the day was to put up drywall in the two upstairs bedrooms. There were sixteen volunteers, and we divided into two teams of eight.

At first, many of us (myself included) were a little nervous and uncertain. I wondered, "Are we really going to cut drywall with an electric saw?" "Do you need a license to operate that thing?" and "How exactly do you put up drywall? For that matter, what *is* drywall?"

Marie truly had a passion for her work. She showed us how to use the saw and put up drywall. I learned that drywall isn't difficult to install, but it's messy. When you cut it with an electric saw, knife, or blade, the material sheds a white, powdery substance. Soon my brown construction boots, my jeans, and

How I got started:

My experience as a certified CPR and first aid instructor (at 17) strengthened my desire to work in my community, break down barriers, and learn from people of various cultural backgrounds.

Accomplishments:

Over the course of two years, our student chapter of Habitat for Humanity built four houses. Currently, I'm cofounding a Habitat for Humanity campus chapter at Barry University in Florida. I was a Coca-Cola Regional Scholar (1994–1998), an Environmental Protection Agency Fellow (1996–98), and the first person to receive a Bronze Congressional Award from the U.S. Congress in the 15th district (Manhattan) for volunteer service (awarded in 1993).

How I stay motivated:

A painting on my bedroom wall reads: "Effort and courage are not enough without purpose and direction." To keep motivated, I remind myself why I'm reaching for a particular goal. My personal philosophy consists of something I call SMEEPS, which stands for Spiritual, Mental, Emotional, Economic, Physical, and Social well-being. When all of these factors are met in my life, I feel in complete harmony with myself and my surroundings.

My future:

My goal is to become a physician and healthcare executive. After I finish graduate school (where I'm studying biomedical sciences), I plan to earn a medical doctorate and master's of business administration (MD/MBA).

the scarf I wore over my head were spattered with white dust. With the exception of my eyes, which were protected by safety goggles, my face appeared to be covered with baby powder.

The labor tired us out, but everyone on the team kept encouraging each other. Neighbors stopped by to tell us to keep up the good work—they also joked around with us, asking if we could help them with *their* houses.

A task that seemed insurmountable at first was completed in just a few hours. Our uncertainty had disappeared, and in its place was a tremendous bond forged between the volunteers, the construction workers, and the family. The work we'd done helped bring the family a step closer to moving into their own home, and we all felt as if we had accomplished something great that day.

Over the next four months, our chapter worked at this site every other Saturday. Our relationship with the family grew stronger, and we all became close friends. The mother spoke at our school, thanking us for our efforts and encouraging us to continue our volunteer work. She was very inspirational, and she gave students at the university a face-to-face look at some-one who had benefited from community service.

I've come to see that building a Habitat house is like raising a child. A baby is born into the world with virtually nothing, not even clothes on her back. What she does have is potential. This is similar to the vacant lots of the building sites: There's nothing but potential.

As a baby is cared for by loving individuals, she begins to develop physically, mentally, emotionally, and spiritually. With the continued nurturing and commitment of parents, family, and friends, the once helpless yet precious child can grow into an independent, productive member of society.

In much the same way, a Habitat house needs nurturing and commitment. It takes the love of people like Millard and Linda

Fuller and the countless volunteers around the world who continue to devote their time and energy to this mission of building homes and building lives.

Getting involved has always come naturally to me, and my commitment to community service will be a part of me forever. In the words of photojournalist Margaret Bourke-White: "Only by his actions can a man make himself/his life whole. You are responsible for what you have done and the people whom you have influenced." Being able to give back, to influence the lives of others in a positive way, is what makes me happy and whole.

Go Exploring

The Kid's Guide to Social Action: How to Solve the Social Problems You Choose—and Turn Creative Thinking into Positive Action by Barbara Lewis (Minneapolis: Free Spirit Publishing Inc., 1998). This award-winning book tells true stories of young people who are making a difference by helping to solve social problems. It's filled with ideas, tips, and resources to help you make a difference, too.

Habitat for Humanity International
121 Habitat Street
Americus, GA 31709
(912) 924-6935
http://www.habitat.org

This nonprofit ecumenical Christian housing ministry seeks to eliminate poverty housing from the world and to make decent shelter a matter of conscience and action. The organization sponsors youth programs and campus chapters to capture the imagination and hope of young people (of all ages, religions, and backgrounds) and to build homes for those in need.

Susie Maroney

---- Open-Water Marathon Swimmer ----

Birthdate: 11/15/74
Hometown: Sydney, Australia
Family: mom, Pauline; dad, Norm; brothers,
Michael (30) and Sean (24—my twin);
sisters, Karin (28) and Lindy (26)
Hobbies: swimming, community service

I love swimming in the ocean. My biggest accomplishments to date are swimming unassisted (meaning no flippers) from Cuba to Florida in 1997 and from Mexico to Cuba in 1998. I set world records both times. These feats have been verified and recognized by the International Swimming Hall of Fame in Fort Lauderdale, Florida.

Swimming land to land had always been my lifelong dream. I knew that other people had tried to swim the Straits of Florida, from Cuba to Florida, but no one had been successful. I made my first attempt in June 1996, but unfortunately, I didn't reach my goal.

During the first four hours of the swim, the rough, choppy seas tossed me around in the custom-built floating shark cage I swam in for protection. As I swam, my wrists slammed against the moving cage so hard that they were both fractured. I had to leave the safety of the cage and its metal bars. For the next eight hours, I swam outside of the cage, surrounded by boats with armed crews in case we encountered sharks.

At one point, a 50 ton sperm whale swam nearby, but it didn't pose a danger to me. However, the whale got playful with one of the boats and came quite close. Joe Pignatiello, the event coordinator, joked that the whale "fell in love" with the boat and was trying to show its affection.

Eventually, I swam back into the cage and continued toward my dream.

Due to an unexpected storm, the currents became too rough for me. I was pulled out of the water thirty-nine hours after the

> "You'll have good days and bad days, but on the bad days you must never think that you've failed."
>
> – Susie

start of my swim—seasick, dehydrated, and exhausted. The worst part was that I was only 12 miles short of reaching my goal.

I spent the next year training harder, swimming six hours at a stretch in the ocean. I also worked on my upper body strength to become more fit for the next try.

On May 1, 1997, I left my hometown of Sydney, Australia, and flew to Cuba for my second attempt. Although I was nervous, I felt positive. Because I'd already attempted the route, I knew what to expect, and this helped prepare me mentally for what was to come.

I'd proven to myself that I could swim nonstop for thirty-nine hours, and I was ready to do it again. I knew that, weather permitting, I wouldn't have to swim much longer than last time. I was anxious to pursue my dream once again.

The marathon swim was scheduled to begin May 8, but due to less than ideal weather conditions, it was delayed forty-eight hours.

On May 11, the sea was calm. It was time to go. I took seasickness pills and put on my swimsuit and bathing cap. My brother Michael rubbed sunblock and petroleum jelly all over my arms and legs to protect me from the sun and harsh water.

At exactly 11:46 A.M., I jumped off the Malecon seawall in Havana, Cuba, into the shark-infested waters of the Straits of Florida.

I made my way into the shark cage that would be my home for the next 107 miles. It was 20 feet long, 8 feet wide, and 8 feet deep. During this attempt, the cage had a windshield to buffer the wind and a canopy to block the sun's scorching rays.

I love the ocean. And I love the little fish that find their way into my cage and swim alongside me. Yet, I'm terrified of being devoured by a marine predator. This is why I'm always thankful for my cage, which helps keep away sharks and other unwelcome visitors.

Two boats accompanied me. One was a tow vessel that pulled the cage; my mom and brother were aboard. The other, an escort boat called the *Reel Lady,* carried the crew members, including Joe, two captains, a navigator, and a doctor. An independent, official timekeeper and observer came along to verify the swim.

All of these people, but especially my family members, provided moral support. They were my constant source of encouragement—cheering me on, telling me how well I was doing, and providing updates on my progress.

The goal was to make an unassisted, continuous swim. I wasn't allowed to hang on to the sides of the cage, get out of the water, or sleep. To rest, I treaded water for a few minutes every hour; a longer break meant the risk of drifting and losing ground. I nourished my body during these short breaks, drinking hot chocolate and nutrient-rich sports drinks, and snacking on baby food, high-protein cakes, yogurt, and chopped bananas.

Getting through the night was the hardest part of my swim. In the dark, the water was so black that I couldn't see a thing. Jellyfish stung me, which was scary and painful. I swallowed a lot of saltwater, which made my tongue swell. I was nauseated, and I vomited a couple of times. I even hallucinated, imagining monkeys hanging on the cage and having a conversation. My mom and my brother took turns leaning by the cage, talking to me so I wouldn't be too lonely or frightened.

Many times, I considered giving up. It's hard to keep swimming when you can't see your destination, day or night. To help beat the boredom, I sang songs in my head, especially upbeat ones by entertainers like Madonna. I also thought about old episodes of the TV show *Seinfeld* to keep my mind occupied. More important, I told myself that my support team was there for me, applauding my efforts and urging me to continue. I just had to keep going—for them and for me.

When I finally saw the morning sun, I was happy and relieved. Another day had come.

Soon I faced a new problem. The shark cage was badly damaged, and about 7 miles from our landing spot, the support cables broke. One of the cage's pontoons, which helped it to stay afloat, had split open and was filling with water.

Joe decided that I should get out of the cage, then suddenly spotted a 10 ½ foot hammerhead shark heading right for me. A few minutes later, crew members noticed an 8 foot blacktip shark. The only option was to repair the cage and continue.

About 100 yards from shore, I swam out of the cage and headed for my destination: Fort Zachary Taylor State Park on Key West. Shortly after noon, I touched sand. I was the first person in history to swim from Cuba to Florida.

I had made the journey in just over twenty-four hours. Exhausted, but unbelievably happy and proud, I realized one thing: My dream had come true.

In May 1998, I set out to break another record, attempting to swim from Mexico to Cuba. I was nervous because this time I'd face the challenge of surviving *two* nights, instead of one.

I knew that the marathon wasn't going to be easy. I tried not to dwell on the miles of open sea that lay ahead, or the pain that I'd no doubt have to endure. Instead, I focused on the positives—like how much I love the water and how good it feels to go for a goal.

Before I could begin the swim, I had to sign

Susie swims in a cage that protects her from dangerous sharks.

papers from the Mexican government, releasing the country from any liability if I were to get injured or killed in the waters of the Gulf of Mexico. Then I was ready to go.

I started the 128 mile swim from Isle Mujeres, near Cancun, Mexico, on the afternoon of May 30. It was a Saturday. This time, I wore a specially designed Lycra skinsuit that was supposed to protect me from the jellyfish (I still got badly stung, though).

My shark cage was towed by a 68 ½ foot shrimp trawler known as the *Prospector*. The first night, the waves were much bigger than what I'd experienced during my previous swim. The

How I got started:

I started swimming when I was three because of asthma. My mother heard that swimming might strengthen my lungs and help relieve some of my asthma attacks. I'm glad she encouraged me to swim; it's been a great confidence-booster and has taught me to set and achieve goals.

Accomplishments:

1998: First person to swim from Mexico to Cuba. 1997: First person to swim from Cuba to Florida; first person to swim from Sydney Harbor to Newcastle. 1996: Record setter for the longest distance swim in 24 hours. 1992: Winner of the Round Manhattan Island Marathon swim race. 1991: Winner of the Round Manhattan Island Marathon swim race; first Australian to swim a double crossing of the English Channel. 1990: Youngest and fastest Australian to swim the English Channel.

How I stay motivated:

I enjoy the challenge of going farther than I did before. A marathon swim is tough, but I stay motivated by thinking about my goal and doing my best to reach it.

My future:

I plan to keep training and challenging myself. When I'm not training, I keep busy with community service, helping to raise money for organizations like the Asthma Foundation and the Special Olympics. I love children, and I want to do everything I can to help kids who suffer from asthma like I once did, or who deserve special recognition and help reaching their goals.

violent seas tossed me about; I swallowed a lot of saltwater, then vomited it up.

Even the support crew aboard the accompanying command vessel, the *Anacay,* became so seasick that they had to be medicated and take vitamins. Due to my nausea, I could only drink small amounts of liquid and eat a little baby food. The bright spot during all this was that I often swam with sea turtles, dolphins, and sailfish.

The first night was difficult. I experienced hallucinations, where I saw a pirate hanging over the cage and fish attacking each other. I felt isolated, lonely, and frustrated. It seemed like I wasn't getting anywhere because I couldn't see land. I was so tired that my eyes kept shutting.

I managed to get through it. And having gone this far, I wasn't about to give up.

When I saw the lighthouse at Cabo San Antonio, located on the western tip of Cuba, I knew that the end was in sight. I had already swam more than thirty hours and had about four more hours to go.

As I finally approached the shore, the waters were too shallow for the shark cage, and I left it behind. The crew was worried about sharks, so my two brothers, who had come along to support me, jumped into the water and escorted me for the last half mile.

At 5:03 A.M., June 1, I reached Las Tumbas beach. I'd spent more than thirty-eight hours in the ocean. I was out of breath, sore, exhausted, and in pain from jellyfish stings, so my brothers helped me out of the water. Setting foot on that beach was one of the biggest achievements of my life.

It felt so good to see my family's faces. I could tell right away how proud they were of my accomplishment. I was just happy that the swim was over. In the process, I had set two more records—the longest unassisted open-water swim and a world distance record for the farthest swim in the ocean.

People often ask me why I would ever put myself through such grueling ordeals. I tell them that I love marathon swimming, and I enjoy the challenge of seeing if I can go a longer distance than before. I also like taking risks, setting goals, and testing my limits.

Sure, it's tough to swim so far, but afterward, I feel great about myself. For me, it's not an ordeal but a way to discover who I am and what I'm really capable of accomplishing.

Go Exploring

Open Water Swimming by Penny Lee Dean (Champaign, IL: Human Kinetics, 1998). This book helps prepare aspiring distance swimmers to reach their goals by offering stretches, training drills, and sample workout programs. It also tells about different open-water events and how to prepare yourself mentally and physically.

The Official Susie Maroney Web Site
http://www.susiemaroney.com/
Log on and meet Susie Maroney. Read interesting facts and details about her open-water marathons, sign her guestbook, and hear about her upcoming swims.

Kristine Denise Ferrer

------------------ Kickboxer ------------------

Birthdate: 2/19/79
Hometown: Los Angeles, California
School: Los Angeles Valley College
Family: mom, Victoria; dad, Manuel; brothers,
Vincent (24) and Manuel, Jr. (22)
Hobbies: math, reading, tennis, in-line skating,
street hockey, swimming

t's amazing what I've learned to withstand since I started training as a kickboxer. In the beginning, I had no idea how much it would hurt to get hit. The first time my coach hit me I was so dazed that I saw stars. I thought, "Wait a minute, I'm a girl—you're not supposed to do that to me!" I stood there like a deer in the headlights. Things sure have changed.

I got into this sport when I saw a sign in a tiny strip mall saying: "Kickboxing." I decided to check it out. The instructor, Richard Batin, taught *Muay Thai* kickboxing, the national sport of Thailand. Accounts of contests in this sport date back to the 1700s.

In Muay Thai, kicks are low and sweeping, with the fighter targeting the knees, shins, and ribs. In addition to punches and kicks, fighters can use their elbows and knees to strike their opponent. The techniques are effective for self-defense and physical fitness training, as well as actual competitive fighting.

From the moment I saw Muay Thai kickboxing, I was mesmerized. The moves weren't artistic or choreographed like other forms of martial arts; instead, they were incredibly intense but practical. I signed up for classes right away.

When I first started going to Batin's Kickboxing Gym, I went to class several times per week. My shins took such a beating from all of the kicking that I wore sweatpants in the summer to hide the bruises from my mom. To build calluses along my shins and toughen them up, I practiced hitting them on the padded bar on the side of the ring over and over again. Now I hardly get any bruises at all, but if I do, it's no big deal to me.

> "The most important thing is to have a dream and not let anything hold you back in its pursuit."
>
> – Kristine

I went through conditioning drills and worked on basic techniques, kicking and hitting bags and pads held by other students.

It didn't take long for me to decide that I wanted to pursue this sport to the next level—competitive fighting. Before I could advance, however, I had to prove myself to my coach and show him that I was dedicated enough to go the distance.

I began training privately with Coach Batin in September of 1997. My workouts became more and more intense, until I was training two to

Kristine *(right)* practices kicks with her coach, Richard Batin.

three hours a day, five to seven days a week. In March 1998, my coach announced that there was a potential fight for me against a girl of about the same weight. I was excited and eager to see what I could do, so the arrangements were made and the fight was officially set up for March 28. I had three weeks to prepare.

Those three weeks were the toughest I've ever experienced. My coach and I trained for three solid hours each day, six days a week, to get me in top fighting form. My workouts, which were already tiring, became even more strenuous.

I started out doing some type of cardiovascular exercise to warm up—usually jumping rope—followed by punching and kicking the bags. Then I went into the ring to spar with either my coach or my boyfriend. (I used to spar with other girls at the gym, but they gave up because it was too difficult.) We'd go seven or eight rounds in the ring, four minutes each, with a minute to rest in between. This was definitely the most grueling part of my workout.

Whenever we'd fight, there was no holding back—the guys punched and kicked me as if I, too, were a guy, and that's just the way I wanted it. I returned the punches and kicks just as hard. This was great preparation for me because I knew that if I could hold my own with an opponent who outweighed me by 40 pounds or more and still remain focused and aggressive, I could fight another girl my size with no problem.

After sparring, I worked with weights to tone my muscles. To strengthen my abdominal muscles, I'd lay on my back, and my coach would stand above me and drop a 20 pound *medicine ball* (a heavy stuffed leather ball used for conditioning exercises) on my stomach. Ouch!

How I got started:

A few years ago, I decided that I wanted to learn martial arts, so I started taking classes in American kickboxing because it looked like fun. American kickboxing uses high, dramatic kicks and flying spins (like what you see in Jean-Claude Van Damme movies). Since I'm only 5 feet tall, I found it nearly impossible to do the high kicks that are such a big part of the sport. I knew that I wanted to do *some* form of kickboxing, but one that was more challenging and satisfying for me personally.

Accomplishments:

I was an honor student throughout high school, did advanced placement coursework during my senior year, and graduated with honors. I played on the North Hollywood High tennis team and was team captain in 1997; my senior year I was undefeated.

How I stay motivated:

What keeps me motivated is what Coach Batin has taught me: Size doesn't matter, and girls can do anything. In his gym, I can be aggressive and strong. There's no discrimination; men and women train together as equals.

My future:

I've always been good with numbers, so I'm studying accounting at a community college, and when I finish there, I hope to get into the University of Southern California (USC). My goal is to continue kickboxing at the amateur level and eventually work my way into the professional ranks.

The match was held at the L.A. Boxing Gym at 8 P.M. When I arrived, the place was filled with people who had come to watch the competition, as well as judges who would score the event.

Each fight has three rounds, lasting two minutes each. You're scored based on how many hits you attempt, along with the number and location of the punches and kicks you land. If you knock out your opponent, you win.

The only protective equipment fighters must wear are head gear and shin guards. I had called ahead of time to ask whether I needed a chest protector, which is optional protection; I was told that I didn't. But when I checked in for the match, the officials said that I *did* need a chest protector. This wasn't good news.

Because I never train with a chest protector, I didn't bring one with me, and the only available protectors were in large and extra-large sizes—I needed a small. My coach began to have doubts about the match, and he wanted to postpone it. But I insisted on going through with it. I thought I was ready.

Turns out, my body was in top form, but my mind and heart weren't. As my coach taped my hands with boxing wraps to prepare me for my turn in the ring, he tried to get me mentally ready. I was nervous, and I knew I couldn't throw hard punches and land them effectively if I was too tense.

In the past, I'd taught myself to relax, so I'd have a clearer sense of my surroundings and could better anticipate moves and blocks. But on the night of my competitive fighting debut, I calmed myself down too much. I couldn't focus; my heart just wasn't in it.

They signaled the beginning of the fight, and I felt as if I wasn't quite awake. After hearing the bell, my thoughts came slowly, "Huh? Fight? What? Oh, okay, here goes. . . . " All I could hear was the sound of the crowd.

My opponent was several inches taller than me, and she outweighed me by at least 20 pounds. There was power behind her kicks and punches, although my adrenaline level was too high for me to really feel their impact. When it came to my own strikes, I kept thinking, "Come on, you can do better than that!"

I landed a few leg kicks that made my opponent buckle, and she even fell a few times. I was amazed that I could get her to move at all, considering our size difference. The chest protector I was wearing practically fell off me, and my mind was screaming, "I can't move with this thing on! I want it off!" I was so distracted that I couldn't fully concentrate on the match.

Round one ended, and my coach called the fight. He thought it wasn't a good situation for me to be in. Unfortunately, that was the moment when I finally managed to get focused. I realized I didn't want to stop.

The other girl raised her glove to signal she'd won, and I wanted to shout, "Hold everything!" It was too late; the match was over. I was disappointed and frustrated, and I felt as if something had been stolen from me.

I know I have much more potential than what I demonstrated in my first match, and I'm hopeful about my future as a kickboxer. I don't let the loss of my first match get me down. In fact, thanks to my training in Muay Thai, I've developed enough confidence to handle whatever comes my way, in or out of the ring.

There's a sign on the wall at the gym that reads: "The only one standing in the way of your goal is you." I know this is true. Any girl can do what I do, but it's not easy. You can't expect to be great when you start out or to master everything right away. Building your confidence and skill level takes time and effort. I'm willing to put in both.

Go Exploring

Check your phone book for a local studio or training facility that offers kickboxing or martial arts classes. If you want to learn more about other forms of martial arts, you can contact the organizations listed on the next page.

American Amateur Karate Federation
1930 Wilshire Boulevard, Suite 1208
Los Angeles, CA 90057
(213) 483-8262
http://www.dallas.net/jka/aakf/aakf.html

This organization is the national federation of karate (a Japanese art that teaches self-defense using hand strikes, chops, punches, and kicks). The federation sanctions events for members and provides referrals to schools.

United States Muay Thai Association (USMTA)
6535 Broadway, Suite 1K
Riverdale, NY 10471
http://www.usmta.com

The USMTA provides a listing of Muay Thai fighters and information about the martial arts. The Web site provides an international Muay Thai magazine; you can enter upcoming events and check out products and equipment.

U.S. Taekwando Union (USTU)
One Olympic Plaza, Suite 405
Colorado Springs, CO 80909
(719) 578-4632
http://www.ustu.com/

Taekwando is a popular Korean art, known for its powerful high kicks; opponents use their hands, feet, elbows, and knees to strike each other. The USTU is the national governing body for the sport and sponsors competitions, state championships, and the Junior Olympics.

Michelle Olson

---- Mountain Climber & Adventurer ----

Birthdate: 2/7/81
Hometown: Astoria, Oregon
School: Astoria High School
Family: mom, Natalie; dad, Rex; stepdad, Donovan; sister, Kathleen (19); brother, Rex (14); stepsister, Chelsey (13)
Hobbies: mountain climbing, listening to all kinds of music, playing the cello

In April of 1997, my friends Morgan, Dan, Bill, and I entered a contest sponsored by *Outside* magazine and the National Outdoor Leadership School (NOLS) to plan the adventure of our dreams. The four of us read about other outdoor adventures, studied maps, and contacted John Roskelley, a famous mountaineer, for advice. He suggested that we climb Mount Sir Sanford, an 11,590 foot glacier peak in the remote area of British Columbia's Selkirk Mountains.

We researched the idea and decided to go for it. Next, we submitted our contest proposal to the judges. We knew the grant would be awarded to the proposal that best combined exploration, conservation, adventure, and potential for success. Our idea was to travel on foot to the Selkirks, explore the landscape and wildlife, and then climb Mt. Sir Sanford in one day. Another goal was to spread awareness of the endangered woodland caribou that live in this remote location. As it turned out, we won the contest!

"Determination and faith keep you going."
— Michelle

The expedition, which lasted about a month, was the most meaningful and wonderful experience of my life. I learned how to kayak, climbed treacherous ice-covered glaciers, and even endured a monstrous five-day *bushwhack* (hike through heavy bush). Facing the challenges of day-to-day survival in the wild helped me discover that I could meet each obstacle with the true spirit of an adventurer.

Highlights from my journal entries tell the story best:

July 5, 1997—I leave my home at 7:30 A.M. and head for NOLS base camp near Olympia, Washington, with my friends. Along with our parents, we drive north with signs plastered on our cars: "NOLS or BUST" "Save the Caribou" and "1997 *Outside* Adventure Grant Winners!" We arrive four hours later and meet the guides (Del and Judd) who will be with us during the journey. Del and Judd are both fun, and they're experienced wilderness travelers. The rest of the day is spent getting familiar with our surroundings and equipment.

July 6—We get our gear ready and begin learning skills for our trip, including how to climb ropes and tie knots. There's so much to learn! I sometimes wonder, "What I am doing here? I don't know anything about mountains." But I'm not about to let a once-in-a-lifetime chance pass me by.

July 7—Our first glacier-training trip takes us up Mount Baker, in the North Cascades of Washington state. I didn't expect climbing with a pack to be like this—it feels awkward, and my feet are clumsy in the snow. What a wake-up call!

July 8—Day two of training. We get up early to make breakfast on little gas stoves. Each of us is figuring out how to adapt. It starts to rain, so we stay in our tents for the remainder of the day.

I hate going to the bathroom because I have to put on all of my snow gear, leave the tent, and find somewhere to go. The boys just open the tent flap and go right outside (no fair!).

July 9—In spite of the rain, we leave our tents to learn new skills like how to hike in the snow and how to use our ice axes. Later, we hike down the mountain, heading back to NOLS base camp.

July 11—Early in the morning, we pack up our gear and head for Golden, British Columbia. We're supposed to camp, but we stay in a hotel due to a heavy rainstorm. Everyone is excited about getting started tomorrow.

July 12—The drive in the van is long, and although we are delayed by a mud slide, we arrive in Golden a day ahead of schedule. We make the final arrangements for our adventure, then set up camp next to a river.

July 13—Two wildlife biologists teach us about the endangered caribou and other animals we may encounter, including grizzly bears.

July 14—The real adventure begins! We pack our gear in kayaks and leave civilization behind. It's a gorgeous day, and the water is *cold*.

Kayaking is hard—I have no experience paddling. It takes us six hours to travel 8 kilometers (about 5 miles). I've struggled all day, and I'm relieved when we stop. We're in a part of Canada that's virtually untouched by humans. It's amazing to see unspoiled landscape. I see the Selkirk Mountains to my left and the Rocky Mountains to my right.

We set up camp on a beautiful rocky beach. Our "kitchen" is located several yards away from our tents, so brown bears and grizzlies (who might smell the food) won't get too close to where we're sleeping. We pack up anything with a scent (food, toothpaste, sunscreen, etc.) so the bears won't be curious. We've been taught that if confronted by a grizzly, we should play dead. A good way to avoid bears altogether is to make a lot of noise and stay in large groups.

For dinner, we make quesadillas with black beans and cheese, one of our favorite meals. Our rations include staples like pasta, dried beans, cheese, peanut butter, and dried milk. We also carry hot drink mixes, a spice kit, and mixes for pancakes, warm cereal, and even cheesecake.

July 15—I've finally mastered kayaking techniques, and it feels awesome (it's not that hard if you do it right). The surface of the water looks like glass, and the weather is perfect.

We reach our campsite and discover that it's unsuitable—the beach is too steep, and there's nowhere to set up tents. We paddle across the lake in open water, which is dangerous because if a storm comes while we're away from the shore, we're vulnerable to tipping and drowning. I start racing the boys and win, which shows how much my stroke has improved.

Everybody is excited. From our new campsite we can see Palmer Creek and part of the Sanford Range, and we know we're this much closer to our destination. After unpacking our gear, we all go for a swim. The lake is freezing, but we don't mind. Morgan, Dan, Bill, and I drag a huge log off the beach and put it in the water so we can float on it. It's a blast!

Even at this early stage of our trip, I'm noticing changes in myself. My confidence is growing every day, and my decision-making skills are improving tremendously. I'm learning so much about being in the wilderness—how to build fires without leaving a trace, how to go to the bathroom in the woods (which is on my top ten list of *least* favorite things to do), and how to wash dishes with pinecones.

July 16—Another long day of kayaking. We paddle into pristine wilderness, where we're completely isolated from other people.

The rest of the trip will be made on foot, so we tie up our boats and leave them there until we can pick them up on the return route of the trip. Judd and Del set up camp. Morgan, Dan, and I scout for a trail up Palmer Creek, which points the way to the Great Cairin Hut. This remote hut was built by the Harvard University Mountaineering Club, and the hikers who stop here use it as a base and help take care of it. The hut is where our group can replenish our food supply and prepare for our ascent of Mt. Sir Sanford.

Bill has dinner ready when we return, a delicious cheese casserole that he invented himself.

July 17—I have my first taste of hell. My pack weighs about 40 pounds and isn't that bad, but the bushwhack . . . all I can say is *ugh!* We're faced with mass amounts of vegetation growing by Palmer Creek—namely devil's club, which stands about 4 feet tall. Almost every inch of it is covered with thorns. The stalk of the plant looks like some type of medieval torture device. Another thorny fiend is known as stinging nettles—the sting lingers, burning your skin for at least five minutes.

Dan and I affectionately refer to Palmer Creek as "The Beast." NOLS promotes "leave no trace ethics" (which means minimizing our impact on the land), so we don't use knives or machetes to cut down the vegetation—it's just us against the plants. Despite the treacherous trail, I enjoy pushing myself.

How I got started:

In March 1997, my friend Morgan and I were in advanced algebra class when he showed me a flyer for the *Outside* magazine contest. We assembled our team and planned the adventure of our dreams.

Accomplishments:

I live in a very small town, and there isn't much to do, so going on this adventure was my greatest accomplishment to date.

How I stay motivated:

All I can say is that if I want to do something, nothing or no one can stand in my way!

My future:

I want to finish high school, then go to Europe for a year and bike through as many countries as I can. After that, I plan to attend college. Morgan, Dan, Bill, and I are also discussing the possibility of another adventure.

July 18—Another torturous day. The local bugs are tasting human flesh for perhaps the first time, and they seem to enjoy the meal—most come back for seconds. Our legs look like hamburger meat. I think we're getting close to our destination, so every cut, blister, sting, and aching muscle is worth the pain.

July 19—I'm learning that you have to keep part of your mind somewhere else while hiking up steep hills and heaving yourself over and under huge fallen trees. My wilderness instincts are growing sharper. Determination and faith help keep me going.

Today I was walking slowly across a tiny dirt ledge on the hillside, and the ground gave way. I grabbed hold of a root and pulled myself up, without thinking twice or screaming. I didn't think much about the incident until Morgan told me that he was impressed with my ability to take care of myself. The days are grueling, but the hard work is bonding us together.

This afternoon, we come across something truly breath-taking, especially to a bunch of tired bushwhackers. It's a huge marsh, with reeds and a wide grove of trees. We're in one of the most remote hiking places in the world. It seems ancient, as if we've leaped back in time to before humans existed. Our team decides to call the area the "Heavenly K" (because it's around a kilometer long).

New rations are being helicoptered to the Great Cairin Hut, and we're scheduled to reach the hut tomorrow. Because the trail food is running low, we stir water into our brownie mix and eat it raw. We're looking forward to a better tomorrow.

July 20—We don't make it to the hut today as anticipated. Due to the warmer weather, glaciers are melting faster than usual, making the local rivers race swiftly and furiously. We need to get across a narrow river, but it's dangerous because the water is running so fast.

Two slippery, slimy logs crisscross the river, and we think it's possible to use them as a way to get over the water safely. Our only other choice is to backtrack down Palmer Creek and take another route, which could add three days to the trip. We take a chance and cross the raging river, walking on the logs. Fortunately, we reach the other side with no difficulty. Then we head for the hut.

We'd better reach the hut tomorrow—all we have left to eat is farina (cereal grains) and Top Ramen Noodles.

July 21—More bushwhacking, then *finally,* we reach a clearing. As we're walking down a ridge, we spot a Canadian Search and Rescue helicopter flying above. (Because we didn't reach the hut on the scheduled date, the authorities thought we had run into trouble.)

The Search and Rescue team seems almost angry to find out that we're okay. Seeing the helicopter and other people makes me realize how different my life is here in the wilderness. No technology, no interruptions. Life has become the mountains, instinct, learning, the team.

We're so close that we can see the hut in the distance. Out of nowhere, a storm erupts through the canyon. Rolling thunder. Bright white lightning. We scramble into action, setting up tents in pouring rain, hail, and hard winds. Nature reminds us who's in control.

July 22—We trek across three rivers and up a huge rocky slope. We're in wet clothes and boots, and we have no food left. The hike is difficult, but we reach the hut. Our food is there!

I'm astounded by the huge ice-covered mountain standing before me, massive in its glory. Mt. Sir Sanford. Blue glaciers loom to my right. I never imagined that something so beautiful existed.

For the next several days, Judd and Del teach us more mountaineering and climbing skills. Soon we'll actually attempt our climb. We camp at a higher elevation to gain some ground. This may save us a few hours on the day of the climb.

July 27—At 3 A.M., Bill checks the weather and shouts, "Wake up! We're going to climb a mountain today!" Because the weather is good, this is the day for the summit attempt.

Everything we've worked so hard for has led us to this point. We know that it's our one chance to make it to the top.

Wide-eyed, we dress and eat a quick breakfast of potato pearls (dehydrated mashed potatoes) and leftover rice. Then we put on our headlamps and start up the mountain, our *crampons* (metal spikes clamped onto our boots) breaking through the crunchy snow.

Brilliant stars and a luminous crescent moon shine in the sky. The snow glows aqua blue in the moonlight, and the mountain stands in the shadows of the cold night. We're on our way.

As we hike, the sun rises, and its warm copper glow illuminates the mountaintop. We continue our ascent, creeping on narrow ledges, climbing along thin cracks in the rock.

We split into two rope teams because it's safer not to travel as one big group. Judd, Bill, and I take the snowy route. Del, Morgan, and Dan take the rocky route. Travel is slow. One slip could mean a long vertical drop onto a snow-covered glacier and, ultimately, death.

Morgan, Dan, Bill, and Michelle sit at the base of "the hourglass"—as far as the group got before deciding to turn back.

At 12:30 P.M., the group meets at the halfway point. We realize that it has taken us eight hours to make it this far. The view from the ridge is spectacular.

The most difficult part of the hike is behind us, but time is running out. It's a very emotional moment.

We hold a team meeting and, as a group, face the grim realization that we won't be able to get to the summit. The top of the mountain is at least a four-hour climb away; it wouldn't be possible for us to reach the summit and climb back down the mountain before nightfall. We face the fact that we need a few more years of mountain-climbing experience to actually make it to the summit in one day. The risk of continuing the climb is too great. We're not willing to give up our lives for the mountain.

We all feel a mix of frustration, disappointment, and pride. We've accomplished so much, yet we're unable to reach our ultimate goal. There are no regrets, only good memories of what we've achieved.

On the mountain today, we connect; we are truly a team.

July 30—Time to head home, back to the everyday grind. This has been the journey of a lifetime. I've tested my limits, pushed myself, and gained a newfound sense of self-respect. I'm now more independent, sure of myself, and prepared to handle whatever life throws my way.

I am not the same girl who embarked on this expedition a month ago: I am changed.

Go Exploring

Outside Magazine
400 Market Street
Santa Fe, NM 87501
(505) 989-7100
http://outside.starwave.com/

Check out the latest issue of *Outside* (at the library or online). You'll find stories, tips on training and nutrition, travel info, and reviews of books and outdoor equipment. If you're online, visit *Outside*'s site to read about various winners of the *Outside* Adventure Grants Contest, including biographies of team members and diary entries from each adventurer. To find out more about the contest, contact: Outside Adventure Grants, Department R, Suite 440, 420 Lexington Avenue, New York, NY 10170. Or call them at (212) 972-4650.

The Mountain Zone
http://www.mountainzone.com
This site, which is affiliated with ESPN, features all sorts of information about mountain climbing, hiking, skiing, snowboarding, and other outdoor sports. Learn about gear, safety, and upcoming events, or check out stories about daring climbs and expeditions.

Veronica Kay

Surfer

Birthdate: 12/8/80
Hometown: La Jolla, California
School: San Diegito Academy
Family: mom, Vanessa; dad, David; stepmom, Celeste; brothers, Rex (23) and Spencer (3); sisters, Natasha (26) and Alexandra (6)
Hobbies: snowboarding, skateboarding, triathlon training, acting

H aving something in your life that makes you feel happy, the
way surfing does for me, is really important. I don't think I
can put into words how it feels to ride a wave. One minute
you're pushing and you feel heavy, and the next you're weightless and free.

It's amazing to glide on the water. When I surf, my whole
body, mind, and soul smile. I smile so big that it almost hurts. I
feel as if I'm connecting with the energy of the ocean . . . it's like
the happiest moment of my life—times ten!

I basically grew up at the beach; our house was only a block
away from the ocean. The first time I got on a surfboard was just
before my fourteenth birthday. I was with Tim Newburn, who's
a friend of the family and like a father to me. He encouraged me
to go for it; suddenly the wave pushed me, and I was up—never
wanting to come down. Surfing offered the challenge and thrill
that was missing from all of the other sports I'd tried. I was
overcome by a feeling of awe. I made up my mind to surf for the
rest of my life.

With its constant ebb and flow, the ocean is a force that
humans can never conquer, tame, or control. When I surf, I feel
in sync with this force. Riding the waves makes me appreciate
the power and magnificence of the ocean.

My mom has been incredibly supportive of my passion for surfing.
One of her girlfriends gave me my first surfboard, a used
8 foot Herbie Fletcher longboard. Another friend of the family,
Peter Curto (a surfer from San Diego), drove me to a local beach
so many weekends and taught me the basics of surfing. I remember winter mornings when it was dark and cold, but we'd still surf.
Many beginners don't stick with surfing for the first winter, but I
did. I loved the ocean, even when the water felt freezing cold.

The following spring, my mom helped me find a surf coach.
One day, the two of us were at a local surf shop, and she started
talking to one of the workers about my love of surfing. He told

her about a young woman named Crissy Jenkins, who ran the North County Girls Surf League. Right away, I knew that I had to meet Crissy. I called her to let her know that I was interested in learning more about surfing. She said that I should come and check out her program.

I began meeting with Crissy and ten other surfers twice a week in Del Mar, California. The league offered me a place to learn new skills and techniques. I felt safe and comfortable among the group.

Crissy made us do sit-ups, push-ups, and visualization (mental imagery) worksheets. As our skills improved, she talked to us about upcoming contests and spent lots of time helping us find our individual style. This way, we'd be prepared to compete.

I soon entered my first surfing contest, which was sponsored by the National Scholastic Surfing Association (NSSA). The event took place at Newport Jetties, a surfing spot in Newport Beach, California. I walked away with the first-place trophy!

I was ready to give this sport everything I had, but money was a problem. The expense of training and traveling for competitions would be a financial burden on my family, but I didn't want to give up. For a while, I worried and felt sorry for myself. But then I realized that you can wallow in self-pity for only so long; it doesn't get you anywhere, and it wastes precious time. I decided that a better approach was to count my blessings and move on.

> "You have to have faith in yourself and the world, grit and determination to stick with it, discipline to stay focused, and most of all, desire."
>
> – Veronica

I've always believed that if you follow the path of your choice and have faith, things will work out for you. My faith has given me the strength to keep moving toward my goals. I believe that God has a plan for me, and by fulfilling my dreams and being a good person, I serve Him. I wrote down what I needed—a way to earn money so that I could help pay for my training and traveling—then I prayed for help.

Veronica catches a wave on her board.

My prayers were answered. At a 1995 NSSA contest, I was approached by a potential sponsor. The company was called Roxy/Quiksilver (Quiksilver manufactures clothes, shoes, and surfing accessories, and Roxy is the girls division of the company). Todd Miller, the team manager and coach for Roxy/Quiksilver, asked me if I'd be interested in joining their team. My answer was a quick YES!

To promote their apparel and equipment, I wore Roxy clothing and displayed a Roxy/Quiksilver sticker on my board when I competed. Soon I began modeling their beach clothes, which led to finding both an agent and other modeling jobs. Suddenly my whole world had changed. I'm living proof that having faith can lead to making your dreams come true.

These days, when I'm asked for my autograph at promotional appearances, I feel embarrassed, flattered, and surprised all in one (I'm still trying to get used to the attention). I feel it's really important for me to give back to the sport in any way I can, so I want to show my support and gratitude. I hope that I'm a role model, and maybe I'll inspire other people to follow *their* dreams.

Two of the greatest things that surfing has done for me is build my confidence and open the doors to other opportunities for success. But surfing has also given me the strength to attack my problems. When it seems like the world is crumbling around me, I go surfing to get a new perspective. Surfing makes me feel happy and positive, and I can sink into these good feelings whenever I'm troubled. Then I'm ready to find solutions.

This has been really helpful for me the past couple of years. My parents divorced when I was five, and I live with my mom. We don't have much money, so I share a bedroom with her, and life isn't easy. My older brother and sister had some serious drug problems, which was hard on all of us. But no matter how tough

How I got started:

I began by just bodysurfing and playing around in the water. Then my dad took me out on his bodyboard. He used to push me into overhead waves at an early age, which was kind of scary at first, but I always ended up okay. This helped me overcome my fears.

Accomplishments:

1998: Seventh place, Oceanside Clarion Pro; first place, NSSA Southwest Conference. 1997: NSSA West Coast Champion; NSSA High School Women's Champion. 1995: NSSA Southwest Conference Champion.

How I stay motivated:

I spend as much time as I can in the water (about 14 hours per week), always ready to catch the next big wave. When I'm not in the water, I watch surfing videos, studying the experts so I can learn their techniques. I also watch tapes of my own performances, which helps me improve my skills. All of this keeps me motivated and in shape.

My future:

I want to be a world champion surfer!

things were at home, I always had surfing. Riding the waves cleared my head and gave me hope.

I learned to stop wishing for a "normal" family and stability; instead, I was thankful for my family because they helped make me the athlete I am today. I've had my share of struggles, but they've made me stronger and more independent. Perhaps if I'd lived a more sheltered or privileged life, I wouldn't be the person I am now. I feel blessed by the lessons I've learned.

Between surfing contests, modeling, and making appearances at stores, my life feels like one big adventure. I now travel so much that I've had to change schools; I go to a local high school designed for students with special skills or needs. I meet with my teachers once a week, and I'm trying to earn credits for my senior year. I'll be graduating a year behind my classmates.

I'm fortunate to have the freedom to pursue my own path, but this also means that I need to be responsible enough to take good care of myself. The pace rarely slows down, but earning the money to pay for travel and competition fees is what allows me to pursue my goals and dreams.

While chasing a dream, you may experience good days and bad days, setbacks and doubts—and you have to be tough enough to handle them. Sometimes you may wonder if it's worth it to keep going, but giving up will probably only lead to regret. If you want to succeed, you need confidence and perseverance. You'll come out on top if you work hard, believe in yourself, and never give up.

I know from experience that you can achieve whatever you set out to do. The world has a lot to offer, so take advantage of the opportunities that come your way. You may be amazed by what you can accomplish.

Connecting with the ocean on my surfboard is the greatest feeling I know. Riding the waves is my passion, my dream, my adventure, my haven. No one can ever take this away from me.

Go Exploring

Wahine Magazine
191 Argonne Avenue, Suite 3
Long Beach, CA 90803
(562) 434-9444
http://www.wahinemagazine.com

Wahine is the girls' guide to surfing and water sports, with photos, interviews, and features. Each month you can catch up on the latest fashions, awesome surf spots, and news in the surfing world.

HI Surf Advisory

http://www.iav.com/hisurfad/

This informative site will give you the latest news on the Hawaiian surfing scene, information about events and competitions, and links to other surfing spots on the Internet. You can also take part in a virtual surfing game and rate your surfing ability, send electronic postcards to friends, watch videos, and check out interviews with surfers.

Surf Diva Surf School for Women
2160a Avenue de la Playa
La Jolla, CA 92037
(619) 454-8273
http://www.surfdiva.com

Surf Diva is an all-girls surf school dedicated to supporting women's surfing. The school offers classes and clinics for all levels and even supplies boards and wetsuits for you to use.

Davida Schiff

------------- Cycling Adventurer -------------

Birthdate: 10/15/84
Hometown: Chicago, Illinois
School: Whitney Young High School
Family: mom, Mardge; dad, Gordon;
brother, Eugene (17)
Hobbies: competitive figure skating,
soccer, tennis, biking

If it weren't for my brother, I never would have gone on the "Girls Rock!" bike trip. My mom originally brought home the brochure about bike adventures for him, but when I read about Girls Rock!, I thought it would be fun. I'm not sure if the trip appealed to me because it promoted self-esteem or because it seemed cool to go biking, rock climbing, and canoeing through New England with a bunch of other girls. All I knew for sure was I wanted to go.

Girls Rock! was a thirteen-day trip organized by a company called the Biking Expedition, which plans all kinds of unique cycling adventures that aim to challenge people and raise their self-esteem. The trip I chose was designed to build new skills, promote confidence, and provide a way for girls to discuss the problems and issues in their lives.

When I was on the plane headed out of Chicago, I started to get a little nervous. It finally hit me that I was really going on this adventure. I realized I had no idea how to mountain bike and had never ridden with heavy gear strapped onto the back of my bicycle.

I arrived in Boston, Massachusetts, scared but excited. There were nine of us in the Girls Rock! group, which was led by two young women named Shannon and Cindy. Shannon was short like me, but she knew how to use her small size to her advantage. (When we were rock climbing, for example, she was able to place her hands in small crevasses and hoist herself up the wall.) Cindy was the experienced biker. She was open, easy to talk to, and fun to laugh with.

"Working together, and helping and cheering for each other, really gives you a sense of what girls can accomplish."

– Davida

Our cycling adventure would take us from southwestern Maine (we'd drive there from Boston), to Sebago Lake in New Hampshire, through New Hampshire's White Mountains, and back to Boston again. I couldn't help but wonder, "Am I really ready for this?"

The first day was the toughest. I wasn't used to biking for so long in a single day, and I really wasn't accustomed to hills (we don't have many of them where I live). The following morning, I woke up *very* achy, and I wasn't sure if I could make it through another day. After we stretched and started moving, I felt better.

We biked about 30 miles each day. I quickly figured out how to change gears on my rented KHS mountain bike, so going up and down hills was easier. I also learned how to ride with supplies on the back of my bike, including a tent, sleeping bag, clothes, food, and cookware. This demanded strength and helped foster a new sense of independence in me. I was learning to become more self-reliant but also discovering the importance of being part of a team.

I still wasn't used to hills, though, and going uphill while road biking tired me out. But then came the fun part . . . going downhill. Once I felt the wind on my face, all the hard work seemed worth it!

Mountain biking was even harder than road biking because of the mud and rocky ground. One day, we rode for miles through the mountains. When we reached the end of the trail, we were totally worn out. We thought we'd covered at least 10 miles and were shocked to find out we'd ridden less than 4.

All of these physical challenges made me really hungry. During the trip, we took turns being on the "cook crew," which meant we'd be responsible for going to the grocery store, buying the food, and cooking it. When we were road biking, we shopped daily because carrying food for more than one day made our load heavier. While mountain biking, rock climbing, or canoeing, we brought enough food for two or three days and stored it in a cooler.

Breakfast usually consisted of cold cereal, orange juice, and fresh fruit. For lunch, we had cold cuts, pita bread with hummus, peanut butter and jelly sandwiches, chips and salsa, and fruit. Throughout the day, we snacked on granola bars, trail mix, and crackers. We usually ate pasta or burritos for dinner, and cookies for dessert. During dinner, we joked a lot and had fun conversations, but afterward we'd take turns sharing the highs and lows of the day. It helped a lot to talk about what we were going through.

Riding along the beautiful New England countryside was relaxing. The only thing I had to think about was the road ahead or what surprises the rest of the day might bring. I wasn't worried about how I looked or what I wore, and neither was anyone else. Some of us even dressed in the same pair of bike shorts every day because that was all we had with us, but no one cared. This made me feel amazingly free.

One of the nicest places we visited was Squam Lake, in New Hampshire, where we went canoeing. We stayed at a large private campsite on an island. Firewood had already been cut for us, and the man who owned the island had built an outhouse for people who stayed there.

In the afternoon, we canoed to Loon Island where some of us swam and others read. That night, I shared a tent with two girls named Ashton and Jaime (on the trip, we rotated roommates each night, so we'd all get a chance to know each other better). The three of us decided to sit by the shore and watch the sun setting behind the mountains. The calm water looked as smooth and untouched as a sheet of glass, except for the water flies that occasionally broke the surface. Everything was so beautiful.

That evening, we played the toilet paper game where you pass around the roll, and each girl tears off a square. For each square, you had to share something about yourself that the rest of the group didn't know. Some of the things people shared were silly, like a favorite food or something that happened when they were little. Shannon and Cindy told us that they "cheated" by starting the campfire with lighter fluid!

Other issues were more serious. We talked about defining sexual orientation, health problems, friends who had committed suicide, difficulties living with step-parents, feeling displaced in the world, and differences between what society says

Davida poses with her bike in New Hampshire.

is "feminine" and what we actually like to do (such as dressing up versus hiking).

Although we spent a lot of time opening up to each other, it wasn't always easy to be supportive and work as a team. The absolute toughest part was rock climbing at the Rumney climbing wall. There were two different areas to climb, so we had to split up into two groups. After my turn, I noticed that the group I was in wasn't cheering for Jaime when she was climbing, so I asked them why. They said they were cheering, just silently. We started to get angry at each other, going back and forth about why people weren't offering support. I got so upset that I just left.

Whenever things got tough emotionally, Shannon and Cindy made us talk about it. The day after climbing the wall, we all discussed our argument. Because the easiest way to judge your success in rock climbing is by how high you climb, people had mixed feelings about the experience at the wall. Some of us felt really good about how far we'd climbed, and others were kind of angry that they couldn't get as far as they'd hoped. All of us were tired after spending about seven hours at the wall, and this made our little fight seem bigger than it really was. After talking about it, we each had to say one good thing about the person sitting to our left, and this helped us all feel better.

Despite any problems we faced, one of the things I noticed about the group was that no one showed off. Everyone felt good when they learned a new task or if they taught someone else a new skill. This really helped boost our confidence.

After each new challenge—road biking, mountain biking, rock climbing, or canoeing—we spent a lot of time talking about a skill we'd used that could help us in other areas of our lives.

How I got started:

I've always been into sports and biking. I've been riding a bike since I was four, and my family has always biked together. It's a family tradition to participate in the Boulevard Lakefront Tour (BLT), which is on Father's Day each year. This tour is a 35 mile bike ride around the boulevards of Chicago. My family also camps, hikes, and mountain climbs together.

Accomplishments:

In 1997, I received the Outstanding Achievement as a Scientist Award (from the Association for Women in Science), and I was captain of the soccer team at the Whitney Young Academic Center. In 1996, I won the History Fair (school, city, and state). In sixth, seventh, and eighth grades, I was the winner of the City Science Fair.

How I stay motivated:

On my Girls Rock! trip, things got tough sometimes. We had to cook our own food, set up tents late at night, ride long distances, and face new challenges all the time. But the group had its own special energy, and this is what helped pull us through.

My future:

I'm thinking about doing a bike trip again, so I can experience another amazing adventure.

For example, I discussed how perseverance was an important skill for me during road biking and mountain biking. When I was struggling to get up a hill, I'd tell myself not to give up. I'd hang on and focus on getting to the top, so I could reach the point where I'd be able to soar down the other side. Now I know I have the perseverance to reach other goals in my life or solve any problems I might face.

At one point during the trip, my perseverance was really tested. We were mountain biking in Gunstock, New Hampshire, on a *really* steep slope. It was my job to be the front leader (the first person to go up the hill). I looked up and got a weird feeling in the pit of my stomach. Then everyone started cheering for me, shouting, "Go Davida! You can do it!"

I decided that I wasn't going to let the hill get the best of me or have to walk my bike halfway up. So I switched into the lowest gear and started pedaling super-fast. It was an amazingly steep slope, but I was determined to make it to the top. I persevered, and when I finally reached the summit, I got off my bike and started cheering for everyone else, whether they were riding or walking.

Throughout the trip, each time I faced a hill, I told myself that if I could just make it to the top, my "reward" would be to coast down the hill. Sometimes I wanted to get off my bike and walk, but I'd tell myself to push harder and keep on going. But this time, in Gunstock, my reward wasn't going down the hill afterward. Instead, cheering for each girl as she made it to the top was the best reward I could imagine. Moments like this helped me feel good about myself.

At the end of the trip, we made a quilt to celebrate our experience, and for the next year, each member of the group gets to keep the quilt for a month as a reminder of all that we shared. While making the quilt, we each had our own square to decorate. I decided to decorate mine with "chain art," which was what we called the grease "designs" we got on our legs from our bike chains. During the first three days of the trip, I had more grease on my legs than anyone, and all of the girls had fun pointing it out to me. So that's what I put on my square—a leg with chain art on it.

I'm looking forward to reliving the trip when it's my turn to care for the quilt. Until then, I know that the greatest reminder of my adventure is my newfound strength, independence, and of course, perseverance.

Go Exploring

The Everything Bicycle Book by Roni Sarig (Holbrook, MA: Adams Media Corp., 1997). Fun, colorful, and easy to read, this book is a great resource for cyclists of any level and age. It includes information on choosing a bike, repairs and maintenance, clubs and touring, proper technique, and equipment.

Girls Rock!
http://www.bikingx.com/girls.htm
If you're interested in a biking adventure trip, check out the Girls Rock! Web site. Created by the Biking Expedition, this unique 13-day trip for girls ages 11–15 allows you to be active, challenge yourself, increase your self-esteem, and grow as a person in a supportive environment. The group does projects such as journaling, murals, and other creative educational experiences while traveling through New England.

Kelly Matthews
------ Aggressive In-Line Skater ------

Birthdate: 1/20/82
Hometown: Hoboken, New Jersey
School: Hoboken High School
Family: mom, Diane; stepdad, Bob
Hobbies: basketball, swimming, soccer

I came down from a trick in the air and was trying to clear the ramp: BAM! I've probably done the trick dozens of times, but this time I tripped. I landed right on my head, which was stinging and burning. Two thoughts crossed my mind: "Will I ever be able to skate again?" and "I hope my face doesn't scar."

Accidents happen in aggressive in-line skating. Fortunately, I was wearing a helmet that day, or my fall could have been a lot worse.

At the time, I was with some friends, and they called the paramedics. Help arrived right away. I was taken to St. Lukes Hospital in Harlem (in New York). Because I was under eighteen, they brought me to pediatrics, where I got twenty stitches over my right eyebrow. Luckily, the scar is hardly noticeable now.

My parents were really upset, but they tried not to show it. My biggest worry was that they wouldn't let me skate anymore.

Kelly performs a trick on the rail box at Chelsea Piers in New Jersey.

The kind of aggressive in-line skating that I do is definitely "extreme." Soaring off a ramp or flying through the air doing a flip or 360 (a vertical spin), I know that I'm risking injury just to entertain myself and the crowd. My parents worry and pray a lot when I'm skating, but they know that I'm dedicated to my sport. I want to do my best because it gives me a great feeling of satisfaction and pride.

My head-slam into the pavement happened in July 1997, just hours after I had placed first in an Aggressive Skaters Association (ASA) event in New York City. The event was called the "B3" for Bikes, Blades, and Boards. A bunch of my friends were at the competition that day, which made it really exciting. With everyone cheering for me, I felt awesome. Adrenaline rushed through me, and the energy I got from the crowd helped me push myself a little harder.

Whenever I'm in a contest, I first check out the course and take a look at how the ramps, rails, and steps are set up. Then I decide on my tricks. At the B3 event, I planned a few 360 spins, plus tricks known as *topside soul grinds* and *royal grinds*. Soul grinds are when you position your skates so the front one is parallel to the rail, and the back one is at a right angle. When doing a royal, you lean your front foot in and your back foot out. (It's kind of hard to describe these tricks—you have to see them to believe them!)

"Positive thinking always pays off."
– Kelly

At skating competitions, the judges score you in four different areas: style, consistency, difficulty, and line. Each skater has a minute to do as many tricks as possible, impress the judges, and fire up the crowd. The great thing about this sport is that all of the skaters are friends—it's about fun, not rivalries. The attitude is: Skate for the thrill of it, and if you win, you win.

Over time, I've gained enough confidence and physical strength to do harder and harder tricks. Aggressive in-line skating is an independent sport; someone can show you how to do a move, but when it comes to learning it, you really just have to practice and practice until you get it right. The more I train, the more fun I have, and the stronger I become.

Concussions and broken wrists are pretty common in this sport. Instead of getting scared, I tell myself to think positive and just go for it. The only way I can master a new trick or reach a goal is by believing in myself 110 percent; otherwise, there's no way I'll be strong enough, mentally or physically, to keep going. Still, no amount of strength and positive thinking can keep someone from getting hurt in a hard fall. Believe me, I've got the bumps, bruises, and scars to prove it!

When I got home after my accident in New York City, I stayed off my skates for about five days, which was tough for me to do. Then I had to get ready to compete again.

At the time, I was in the middle of the ASA Pro Tour, a series of events that run from March to October. You earn points based on how you place in each event, and the combined total of all the points earned on the tour determines your overall ranking.

Despite my injury, I was determined to keep competing. I was a little scared after falling on my head, but I told myself that the only way to lose my fear was to focus on my tricks and the contest. I guess it worked because I came in first place! The points I earned from all of the combined ASA events ranked me third in the world.

Nothing can stop me from doing what I love. I've been injured while skating on other occasions, like when I broke my wrist doing a trick on a rail at Toms River Park in New Jersey. A week later, I was back on my skates, cast and all.

I'm really proud of all that I've accomplished. This sport has proven that I have the guts, stamina, and strength to keep going—no matter what happens.

Since 1995, I've participated in everything from local skate-shop contests to the X Games (the "Alternative" or "Extreme" Olympics). I've traveled all over the country—from hot, beautiful beaches to cold, rainy cities. It's been an amazing experience, especially considering my age, and I try to enjoy every moment.

Being away from home, touring different cities, and meeting people from all over the world has taught me to be more responsible. I'm on my own a lot, so I've learned to take care of myself in different situations. This makes me feel proud and lucky at the same time.

I try to support aggressive in-line skating any way I can, so I can give back to the sport that has given so much to me. I've participated in photo shoots, videos, and magazine articles, and I've even judged competitions. I'm grateful for all of these opportunities, and I can't wait to see where the sport takes me next.

I know the future holds great things in store, and I have so many goals I want to accomplish. My biggest one? To become one of the greatest skaters in the world!

How I got started:

I've been street skating since 1995, when my friend Dillon introduced me to it. Now I train after school at least four or five days a week. I go to skate parks in the Bronx, Manhattan, South Jersey, and at Camp Woodward (in Pennsylvania)—wherever I can!

Accomplishments:

I'm a full-fledged member of the ASA Pro Tour and have four sponsors: FR Progressions (wheels), Kramer (helmets), Warp (protective gear), and Salomon (skates). I placed first in two consecutive ASA events in 1997 (in New York City and Boston), and the points I earned from all of the combined ASA events I entered ranked me third in the world that year. In 1998, I was named the World Champion of the ASA Pro Tour Women's Street In-Line Skating Competition.

How I stay motivated:

The adrenaline rush I get from aggressive in-line skating is the greatest feeling I know. Not only do I get a major thrill out of competing but also from training. Some people consider training hard work. Not me! I love practicing. Another thing that motivates me as a skater is the fact that many people look up to me and consider me a role model because of what I've achieved.

My future:

I'd like to pursue the ASA Pro Tour for as long as I can and maybe even make it my career. But I know it can't last a lifetime, so I plan to go to college and learn some other skills (maybe veterinary medicine or business). Also, I'd love to travel to Australia, whether I'm skating there or not.

Go Exploring

In-Line Skating by Mark Powell and John Svensson (Champaign, IL: Human Kinetics, 1997). This book covers everything from in-line basics (what kind of skates to buy, safety gear you'll need, where to skate, rules of the road, how to stop and turn) to more advanced aspects of the sport (roller hockey, in-line racing, and aggressive in-line skating).

In-Line Skater Magazine
P.O. Box 53288
Boulder, CO 80323
1-800-727-7728
This magazine includes interviews with skaters, information on the latest equipment, and general tips on skating techniques.

ESPN X Games
http://espn.go.com/extreme/xgames/
Log onto this Web site to get the latest info on the X Games, including a list of alternative/extreme events and interviews with athletes. You can learn about different extreme sports and the lingo used, and get a brief history of the X Games.

Hannah Thomas

---------- Antarctic Researcher ----------

Birthdate: 5/2/77
Hometown: Saratoga Springs, New York
School: Mount Holyoke College
Family: mom, Barbara; dad, John; sister, Rebecca (24)
Hobbies: traveling, hiking, biking, canoeing
in the Adirondacks, writing, reading, gardening

What do you see when you imagine Antarctica? Penguins? Snow? The South Pole? A land covered by ice? Do you see . . . yourself?

It was my dream to go to Antarctica and see for myself what it was like, so I applied for the Antarctic Research Project scholarship, a project cosponsored by the Girl Scouts of the U.S.A. and the National Science Foundation. When I received a phone call from the Adirondack Girl Scout Council (my home council), the message said I'd been accepted—I listened to only half of the message and ran out of my dormitory to tell my friends the news!

I have to confess that I was a bit scared. Was I ready to spend ten weeks living a few continents and an ocean away? Would I be able to understand and participate in all that Antarctica had to offer?

I am, admittedly, a geology major, which means that I study the earth. I say "admittedly" because my sister and I spent so much of our childhood denying the fact that geology existed. You see, our parents are both geologists, and my sister and I resolved to never grow up to have such a "boring" career (little did we suspect that we would both major in geology at college!).

Science. The word has so many meanings. It can be intimidating or overwhelming, sterile in its precision, or even threatening. It can signify the exploration of the unexplored, or the reinterpretation of phenomena already known but not fully understood. For me, science is all of the above, but most of all, it is *discovery*.

"Opportunities pop up everywhere—you just have to grab them."

— Hannah

I want to know why the rounded humps of the Adirondack Mountains, rising near my hometown of Saratoga Springs, New York, look so different from the high, pointed Sierras in

California. I fell in love with the kind of science that allows you to go out and gather information, then bring it back to the lab to decipher its meaning. This is why I was so excited to pack my bags for Antarctica and embark on the opportunity of a lifetime.

October 15, 1997 (my departure date), couldn't arrive fast enough. I flew to Auckland, New Zealand, then to Christchurch, where the United States Antarctic Program is centered. I rested for a couple of days, then departed for Antarctica, this time in a U.S. Navy C-141 transport jet. We took off and, five hours later, I stepped from the jet's dim, cramped interior to an icy runway just outside of McMurdo Station.

The largest of three U.S. research bases in Antarctica, McMurdo is located on a volcanic island known as Ross Island in McMurdo Sound. McMurdo Station contains research labs for onsite research but also supports field-based projects. Researchers and support staff often stop at McMurdo before heading to the South Pole or to other remote field locations.

My boots squeaked on fine snow, my nose crinkled in the fresh chill of air, and I was grateful to be wearing sunglasses to protect my eyes from the bright sunlight reflecting off the Antarctic snow. *Antarctica!* I couldn't believe I was actually there. It was amazing to travel from New Zealand, with its shades of green and brown and its colorful spring flowers, to a place where all you could see was the white of the snow, the blue of the sky, and the muted browns and grays of the land.

The air of Antarctica smelled fresh and unused, so different from the air at home. Back in New York, the damp autumn air was heavy with the sweet scent of rotting leaves. But in Antarctica, the air was cold as it entered my lungs—so cold that it seemed to hold no scent.

The landscape of Antarctica, with its lack of color and its crisp, cold air, may seem harsh, but its beauty is so pure. There are no trees to soften the outline of a mountain range and no flowers on the ground to distract the eye from the clear blue of the sky. Everything is simple and rugged—this is its allure.

In Antarctica, McMurdo Station was my home for ten weeks. I lived in a dormitory, where I had a bedroom and a roommate. From my doorway I could peer at the sea ice and the snowy mountaintops (just in case I should ever forget to be amazed by my new surroundings). Outside, the wind blew constantly, icicles hung from the roof, and, with the windchill, temperatures dropped far below zero.

Staying warm and dry in Antarctica was essential. The National Science Foundation made sure that everyone involved in the project had the proper clothing: I became the proud borrower of two pairs of long underwear, six pairs of wool socks, half a dozen gloves and mittens, a pair of fleece pants, a jacket, snow pants, a heavy down parka, plus hats, hats, and more hats. I was also issued a purple neck "gaiter"—a tube of warm, fuzzy material designed to be worn around my neck (like a scarf) so the cold winds couldn't blow into my jacket. I received a pair of "bunny boots," which were huge white boots that trapped a pocket of air between two layers of rubber to keep my feet warm (so warm, in fact, that they made my feet sweat).

Wet, sweaty socks led to cold feet, and cold feet led to a grumpy me. One of the sayings around the station was: "Change your socks. Change your attitude!" It worked.

My first real adventure in Antarctica was snow school. My roommate, Michelle, and I joined a group of twelve people to learn the basics of survival in the cold. The instructors taught us how to stay warm, avoid frostbite, light a stove, and use a shortwave radio. Then our group was sent on an overnight trip in the snow, so we could practice what we'd learned.

We made a shelter called a snow mound, which was the closest I've ever come to creating an igloo. To make the shelter, we shoveled packed snow on top of a pile of duffel bags filled with sleeping bags, and once the duffel bags were covered by two feet of snow, we dug a hole in the side of the mound and pulled the bags out. *Voilà!* A hollow room was created in the mound.

We spent the rest of the day digging into our snow mound, hollowing out the inside room to make it larger. Vapor from my breath froze to my glasses as we sawed into the hard-packed snow and made snow blocks, which looked like giant sugar cubes. We used the snow blocks to build a wall to protect us from the blowing snow, then set up our two-person tents. By 8:30 P.M., our group had eaten a quick dinner and gone to bed.

I awoke later, listening to the wind as it whipped around the

Hannah stands by a sign that marks the geographic South Pole.

tent, forcing snow through the zippers and coating my sleeping bag in a layer of white. The sun was shining. "Could it be morning?" I wondered. Clock time became fuzzy because Antarctica's twenty-four hours of sunlight made it difficult to know when night turned into day. I looked at my watch: 1 A.M. Burrowing into my sleeping bag, I thought about whether to leave my cocoon in search of the outhouse. Sleep and warmth won out.

When we returned to McMurdo Station, the first day with my science group was "garbage day." We sat on the floor with garbage cans and separated recyclable paper, metal, cardboard, and plastic from hazardous wastes like batteries. By "packing out" our garbage like this, we helped to preserve the environment of Antarctica. (Antarctica is the cleanest continent on earth, and we wanted to keep it that way.)

How I got started:

I've been a Girl Scout for as long as I can remember. Girl Scouts of the U.S.A. helped sponsor my trip.

Accomplishments:

I've given presentations about my Antarctic experiences to elementary schools, Girl Scout troops, Rotary Clubs, and Kiwanis Clubs. Currently, I'm a teaching assistant for the environmental geology lab at my college and a writing assistant at my school's writing center. In 1997, I was nominated as a Sarah Williston scholar for ranking in the top 15 percent of my class.

How I stay motivated:

I was inspired by the chance to break away and define myself. When I knew that I was headed to a remote part of the world, I was itching to see if I could do it. My connections to my family and mentors are very strong, and always will be, but I wanted to do something on my own and prove to myself that I could succeed.

My future:

This experience has made me ready for the next step. Coming from a family of geologists, I had to find out if I love geology without my family around—and I do! Someday I may run a nature center or become a park ranger or teacher.

Once a year, a large ship docks at McMurdo Station, bringing a year's worth of food and supplies from the United States; on the return trip, its decks are filled with the garbage produced by the station. I learned that 70 percent of McMurdo Station's waste is recycled in the United States (the remaining 30 percent is burned at an energy-producing plant in the U.S.).

If you want to know what it was like to "pack out" garbage, imagine taking a two-month road trip and keeping all of your garbage in the car to recycle when you got home. The smell was horrible!

At the station, sewage was released into Winter Quarters Bay (part of McMurdo Sound). Natural wastes dumped into the water added nutrients to the ecosystem, but if the waste had too many metals, it could do damage. Our research team studied how the organisms living in the bay's mud responded to the sewage. We dug samples of mud, took them back to the lab, and strained the organisms. Then we added organic material (food for the creatures living in the mud) and metals.

The next step was for trained scuba divers to place the mud trays back on the sea floor. I helped the divers pack their gear and load the bags and the dive tanks onto the Spryte (an orange vehicle that looked like a cross between a small tank and a pickup truck). The vehicle bounced and jostled over the frozen sea to the dive hut at Cinder Cones, a site for diving and exper-imentation. This was where our real work began.

The only way to get to the ocean floor was by going through a hole melted into the ice. Michelle was a diver on this project, and she told me that diving beneath the ice was like sinking down a long, long tube, then *WHOOM* you're out of the dive hole and into the sea below. The ice roof loomed above her head, and all around her were bright orange sea stars, a form of marine life. A video camera was set up on the seafloor, so researchers like me could view the sea stars and experience the under-ice world, too.

The mud trays placed on the seafloor would stay there for one year. Then they would be dug up and examined, so researchers could find out which organisms had moved into the "polluted" trays and how the waste affected them. The results of this study would help the researchers determine whether it was necessary to build a plant to treat sewage from McMurdo Station.

I had a chance to examine some year-old mud trays brought up fresh from the seafloor. Using a microscope, I studied the mud's surface, which was filled with dozens of short, fuzzy tubes, making it look like a shaggy brown carpet. Worms lived in the tubes, and every now and then, my eye caught one sliding in or out of its "house."

I searched the tray for other life, and I found tiny anemones and *Edwarsia meridionalis,* which looked like bedraggled flowers in an undersea garden. I spotted a pink crustacean that resembled a tiny shrimp wandering among the Edwarsia. Scuttling back and forth on multiple legs, it reared and touched one of the anemone's tentacles. In a flash, the anemone leaned toward the crustacean, grabbed it, and disappeared into the mud. The life in my dish of mud appeared fragile and delicate, but it had the strength to survive and thrive in the icy depths.

My first adventure away from McMurdo Station was flying to Siple Dome in a ski-equipped LC-130 Hercules plane, designed to land on ice and snow. Siple Dome is a field camp on the West Antarctic ice sheet in the middle of nowhere. Here I experienced a lot of firsts—my first time driving a snowmobile, my first time in a field camp of seventy people, and my first glimpse of the huge drills that pull ice cores from the ice sheet for paleoclimate analysis. By analyzing the chemistry of the air bubbles captured in the ice sheet, researchers could determine what the earth's atmosphere was like hundreds of years ago.

My stay at Siple Dome also marked my first Thanksgiving away from home. At the camp, we had all of the usual treats, including turkey, stuffing, and lots of pie. The only thing missing was our families.

Next on my agenda was a week at the Amundsen-Scott South Pole Station. We flew over the Transantarctic Mountains to get there. I'd been told before that ice moves (glaciers, or large bodies of ice, spread across the earth's surface, slowly scraping and reshaping the land). But it wasn't until I flew over these glacial mountains that I realized that ice MOVES. It was incredible to see rumples of ice spilling over the slopes like a slow-moving waterfall.

I thought it was definitely worth standing out in the freezing cold of the South Pole to be introduced to the world of atmospheric science and astronomy. I have to admit that these subjects intimidated me a bit (okay, a lot!), but they amazed me, too. The researchers at the South Pole shared their time and work with me, helping me to understand such things as lasers and the birth of stars.

In mid-December, I visited the penguin colony at Cape Royds on the tip of Ross Island. I had a chance to work with the Adélie penguins, which are about knee-high and have black backs, white stomachs, and a ring that sometimes shows around their eyes. I helped band the birds with radio transmitters, so the researchers could find out where in the ocean the penguins hunt and how much food they bring back to their offspring.

I was able to walk around the penguin colony, watch their various behaviors, and hear their sounds—squawks of penguins in conflict and the patter of feet as hungry birds went to sea to fish, and others returned to the nest with full bellies.

I heard the trumpeting sounds that accompany an "ecstatic display," which is when a penguin stands straight and tall, its flippers outstretched and flapping slightly. With its head tilted to the sky, and its bill straight up in the air, the penguin begins to make a thumping sound that starts in its chest. Soon the bird adds vocalizations that sound like *graak! graak! graak!* and other birds are inspired to join in; the joyous sounds build to a crescendo, and it's a noise like no other. Yet, my favorite sound of all could only be heard beneath the noises of adult members of the colony . . . the soft peeps of the penguin chicks.

I spent Christmas in the dry valleys, one of the few places on the Antarctic continent not covered by snow. The dry valleys are a feast for the eyes because glaciers sort of "drip" off the mountainsides and appear to be suspended from the valley walls. This was my chance to be face-to-face with a real glacier.

It was my first Christmas away from home. We strung Christmas lights, and while we put dinner on the table, I kept waiting for the sun to set so we could turn on the lights. (Silly idea! The sun doesn't set in December in Antarctica.)

Our meal was quiet but wonderful. We were supposed to have fresh food and treats flown in from McMurdo Station (via the "Santa Flight"), but the weather turned bad and the plane couldn't travel safely. We made do with ham, mashed potatoes, carrots, and, of course, pie—lots of pie and a package of cookies, too.

Christmas marked the beginning of the end of my stay. I worked with two more groups of scientists over the next couple of weeks, learning about weather prediction and hunting for fossils from the Jurassic period. Soon I'd be returning home.

On January 15, my plane left Antarctica. I was happy to be going home to see my family, but I felt a pull back to the ice. Looking out the window, I thought about a memorable event that had occurred on my second-to-last night in Antarctica.

It was midnight, I'd been packing, and I was really tired. One of my friends mentioned that some minke whales were surfacing in the ice near the station. I almost didn't walk out to see them because I felt so weary, but curiosity prevailed.

The minkes were surfacing in a hole in the ice, the sun glistening off their backs as they rolled through the water. It was quiet sitting there on the point, straining my ears to hear the intermittent whoosh of a whale taking in air and expelling it. I contemplated the amazing sites I'd seen and all of the new people I'd come to think of as friends.

At the end of my journey, I was thankful that I'd been given a unique chance to get to know Antarctica as a continent, a landscape, and a friend. I understood that I was in love with that beautiful snowy land. I wanted to know more about the forces that shaped it, the life that has adapted to it, and perhaps even what it could teach me about myself.

Antarctica helped me realize how I've grown, and will continue to grow, throughout my life. What I did there, I did on my own. For a short time, I stood alone, unsupported, without my family to cheer me on—and I was able to handle it. Although I don't know where my life will take me, I know I have the strength to keep growing, learning, and seizing the opportunities that await.

Go Exploring

Polar Dream: The Heroic Saga of the First Solo Journey by a Woman and Her Dog to the Pole by Helen Thayer (New York: Delta, 1995). Want to learn more about surviving in arctic conditions? Fifty-year-old Helen Thayer braved frigid temperatures to become the first woman ever to ski solo to the North Pole, accompanied only by her dog, a black husky named Charlie. This is her first-person account of the struggles, hardships, and triumphs during their incredible twenty-seven-day adventure.

Just 4 Girls Web site
http://www.girlscouts.org/girls
Sponsored by the Girls Scouts of the U.S.A., this site offers tons of tips, stories, Q & A sections, games, and ideas to inspire and entertain you. You'll find information about their new initiative, *GirlSports,* as well as health and fitness tips, book reviews, a pen-pal network, an advice column, science and technology news, self-help information, links to other sites for girls, and much more. For more information about Girl Scouts, contact: Girl Scouts of the U.S.A., 420 5th Avenue, New York, NY 10018; 1-800-GSUSA4U (1-800-478-7248).

United States Environmental Protection Agency (EPA)
http://www.epa.gov/students/
On this official Web site for the EPA, you can gain valuable insight on health and safety issues (like pesticides and drinking water, global warming, ozone depletion, acid rain, and hazardous waste). The site also provides lots of great ideas for science projects, how to obtain brochures on conservation and the ecosystem, tips for recycling, and information about environmental careers and internships.

PART 2:

How to Be Gutsy Yourself

In Part 1, you met some remarkable young women who are making their dreams come true. Maybe you want to reach for your dreams, too, or set out on an adventure of your own. Part 2 of this book is about making sure your mind and body are ready for the challenges that lie ahead. You'll learn about the importance of having high self-esteem, setting goals, being fit, taking care of yourself inside and out, and much more.

Getting Your
Mind in Shape

Courage, confidence, optimism (positive thinking)—maybe you weren't born with these qualities, but you can *develop* them. You can also learn to believe in yourself and set goals.

In this section, you'll find seven tips for mentally preparing yourself to succeed: (1) build your self-esteem, (2) be positive, (3) be confident, (4) set goals, (5) visualize your dreams, (6) show courage, and (7) be determined. You might want to use a special journal for the activities included in the "Take Action" exercises.

#1 Build Your Self-Esteem

One of the greatest gifts you can give yourself is self-esteem. This is the belief that you have value just for being you.

When you have high self-esteem, you:

- feel good about who you are

- take pride in your unique qualities and experiences

- treat yourself with honesty, kindness, and respect

In other words, you have a strong sense of self-worth. You have faith in your abilities. You believe in yourself.

Building a good relationship with yourself is an important part of growing up. When you care about yourself, you have a stronger foundation from which to explore your interests, goals, and dreams. You feel more secure about your choices and are more accepting of your mistakes. And you learn to value your

208

individual thoughts, ideas, and opinions—instead of always trying to please other people or live up to their expectations.

What if your self-esteem is only so-so or pretty low? It's time
to turn your thinking around. Instead of putting yourself down,
focus on your good qualities and consider what makes you special. Talk to someone you trust (a parent, friend, teacher, or
counselor, for example) about why you feel like you don't measure up; ask for advice on ways to increase your self-esteem.
You can also check out the "Go Exploring" resources on pages
222–223, many of which focus on girls' self-esteem.

Take Action

The following exercises can help boost your belief in yourself. Pull
out your journal, or a blank sheet of paper, and your favorite pen—
it's list time.

- The next time you put yourself down, saying things like "I wish I were
  someone else" or "I'm not as good as so-and-so," list these criticisms on
  paper (call it your Thought-Pollution List). You don't need all this garbage
  in your head, so tear up the list into tiny pieces and toss them in the trash.
  Do this exercise as often as you'd like.

- Now make a list of all your talents and positive qualities—anything and
  everything that's special about you. Be sure to include what you're good at
  (like music, art, sports, or schoolwork), your strong personal traits (like
  being thoughtful, trustworthy, outgoing, or caring), and your accomplishments (like doing community service or learning a new skill). If you tend
  to be your own worst critic, you may have a hard time thinking of what to
  write; ask family members or friends for their input (you may be amazed at
  the great things they have to say about you). Any time self-doubt pulls you
  down, find your list and read through it for an instant self-esteem boost.

#2 Be Positive

Positive thinking can help you accomplish just about anything. A
positive attitude goes hand in hand with self-esteem, and when

you have these two qualities, you're more motivated to try new things. Who knows? You just might decide to catch a wave on a surfboard, ski down a steep slope, travel to a foreign country, learn to sail, or do something else that captures your imagination.

A positive attitude will help you:

- make the choice to be enthusiastic about life
- stay optimistic (look on the bright side)
- see problems or obstacles as learning experiences
- be a good sport, whether you win or lose
- trust in the future and look forward to it

The great thing about attitude is that *you* get to decide if yours is going to be positive or negative (it's one thing in your life that's *completely* within your control). Your attitude determines the choices you make each day and how you feel about what happens to you.

The key to going after what you want (and getting it) is believing in a positive outcome. When you think the best will happen, it often does. Give positive thinking a try—you may be surprised at how well it works.

If your head is spinning with thoughts like "I won't make the team so why try out?" or "I'll never be good enough," it will be much harder for you to tackle life's challenges. How can you expect to reach your potential if your mind is full of doubt?

Besides, if you're convinced you'll never succeed, you might prove yourself right—this is known as creating a *self-fulfilling prophecy*. You tell yourself you can't do something, so your attitude is "Why bother?" and you don't push yourself to achieve. The result? You don't accomplish what you set out to do, confirming your belief that there was no way you'd succeed.

If you tend to be a negative thinker, do yourself a favor by learning to turn your negative thoughts into positive ones. Negative thinking is self-defeating; it limits your chances for success.

Any time your inner critic steps in and says things like "You can't do it" or "You're no good," tell this faultfinder to take a hike. Push the negative thoughts away and replace them with positive ones. Tell yourself "I can do it," and "I *will* do it," and "I deserve it!"

Maybe you're afraid to try new things because you worry about being embarrassed if you don't succeed. Many people feel this way, so you're not alone. It's difficult to perform in front of others, risk failure when you know people are watching (and even when they aren't), and face potential disappointment. On the other hand, it feels great to try something new and find out what you can do. Giving something a try is the only way you'll ever prove to yourself what you're capable of.

What happens if you think positive but don't succeed at what you hoped to do? For example, suppose you tell yourself you're going to hit a home run in the big softball game but then don't. Instead of getting mad or frustrated, ask yourself how an optimist would handle the situation. Someone who has a positive attitude might realize she had a great time playing in the game and did her best. She'd learn from her errors and think of ways to improve her hitting in tomorrow's game . . . after all, there's always a next time. You can learn to think this way, too.

Changing your attitude requires time and practice every day, so be patient with yourself during the learning process. If negative thoughts pop into your head, don't panic or get angry with yourself. Be aware that recognizing your negative thought patterns is a big step toward making changes in your thinking.

Take Action

Attitude can have a big impact on whether you succeed or fail, so why not think like a winner? If you want to become a more positive thinker, try the following exercise.

Make two columns on a page in your journal or on a piece of paper; label the left side "Negative Thoughts" and the right side "Positive Alternatives." For the next three to five days, keep a list of your negative thoughts, recording them in the left-hand column. Then immediately write a positive counter-statement in the right-hand column. This will help you get in the habit of dismissing negative thoughts and framing them positively.

Here are some examples:

Negative Thoughts:	Positive Alternatives:
"I'm not talented enough to try out for the school play."	"Tryouts could be fun. I might meet new people and learn new skills."
"I don't like my legs. They're too short/fat/skinny."	"My legs are strong, and they help me run, jump, climb, and stay on the move."
"My life is a bore. It will never be exciting."	"Life has many fun things to offer—it's up to me to find activities I enjoy."

#3 Be Confident

When you're confident, you trust in your ability to do something well. You approach a challenge, a task, or an activity with the feeling that you can handle it.

Being confident means you:

- approach new challenges with a willingness to try, even if the outcome isn't guaranteed

- feel comfortable being a self-starter or leader

- express your ideas, opinions, and needs

- can push past self-doubt when facing a hurdle

- are strong enough to stand your ground

- bounce back when things don't go your way

Do you remember when you first learned to ride a bike? You may have had the help of training wheels or the steadying hand of a parent or an older sibling. You probably wobbled and fell, but you kept trying because you were determined to ride on your own. Eventually, you became more secure, and one day, as if by magic, you *were* riding on your own—no longer able to recall how it felt when you couldn't. Throughout the process, you kept trying because you felt confident that you'd eventually be able to ride with all the other kids.

Learning to ride a bike is like many other challenges you might face in life, even climbing mountains, traveling to new places, or trying an extreme sport (or any sport). You'll never learn how if you don't try, and once you succeed, you'll feel a satisfying sense of accomplishment. Each success can lead to another, making you stronger and more secure about yourself— in other words, more *confident.*

Every time you stretch your boundaries or clear a major hurdle, you pave the way for another, bigger challenge. Who knows what amazing things you're capable of achieving on the sports field, at school, in your community, or any other place where you want to make a difference!

Take Action

This exercise is about building your confidence. At the top of a page in your journal or a piece of paper, write "Things I've Tried." Now list any activities you've recently explored or positive changes you've made in your life. For example, write down sports you've tried out for, the name of a new friend, a hobby you started, a Web site you discovered, skills you've improved on, new places you've visited, or anything else that comes to mind. Next to each entry, name at least one thing you learned from the experience.

Here are some examples:

1) tried out for track (and made it!)   learned that I can perform under pressure

2) volunteered at a preschool   found out how much I love helping kids

3) started a yoga class   discovered muscles I didn't even know I had!

The next time you feel like you aren't moving forward or are a little uneasy about trying something new, read the list to remind yourself that life is full of challenges and fun things to learn and try.

#4 Set Goals

If you want to make your dreams come true, where should you begin? The best place to start is with a goal.

What's so important about having goals? Goal setting:

- helps you become more self-assured and self-reliant

- motivates you to achieve the things you want to do

- puts you in charge of your life

- gives you a sense of direction and purpose

Your goals should be things *you* want to accomplish, not what your friends, parents, or coaches tell you to do. Your goals are very personal—they represent what you believe in, want to see happen, and are willing to work hard to achieve. As you think about a potential goal, ask yourself if it's truly important and meaningful to you. What do you really want to achieve?

Once you've decided which goals you'd like to reach, write them down. Putting goals on paper makes them seem more real. (See "Take Action" on page 216 for tips on writing about your goals.)

When you make your list, separate *long-range* goals from *short-range* goals. Long-range goals—the BIG ones—are things you'd like to accomplish far in the future (in, say, five or ten years). Your short-range goals are the small but meaningful steps that lead you to your big goals.

For example, if earning a black belt in karate is your long-range goal, you need to set smaller milestones along the way. You have to find a martial-arts class in your area, take lessons, practice your skills, and gradually earn the various other belts until you receive the ultimate honor of the black belt. Achieving a goal like this doesn't happen overnight—it may take years of hard work.

Every accomplishment starts with a single step, so it's important to begin with *one* short-range goal that will launch you on your way. Start with a goal that's small, manageable, and within reach; then create a specific plan of action so you know how to proceed. For example, instead of setting a general goal to "take a karate class," plan to "visit at least two karate studios this weekend." Now you have a goal that's specific enough to attain.

Next, prioritize the steps you need to take to reach your goals. For each short-range goal, set a target date to aim for. If you meet the goal on the day you planned, celebrate! Do something special for yourself to recognize your efforts.

If you don't reach your goal, figure out why. Do you need extra time, training, help, or resources? Determine what you need and try again. Keep detailed, written records of your progress. Consult your records often—once a day (best) or once a week (minimum). This will help you stay focused and on track.

Even if you follow a detailed plan of action, you may experience a setback. (This can happen to anyone.) The key is knowing how to handle it. Instead of giving up, think of the setback as a red flag alerting you to areas of your plan that need more work. Identify what caused the setback and how you can adjust your strategy so it's more effective. For example, your goal may be too vague or unrealistic. Once you identify the problem, write about it, come up with at least one solution, and give it a try.

If you consistently fall short of your goals, it may be time to reevaluate them. Ask yourself the following questions:

- Are my goals too big?

- Am I truly committed or have my priorities changed?

- Have I made any progress at all?

- Is there someone who can give me a new perspective on my goals and my plans for reaching them?

- Am I having fun in the pursuit of my goals?

- Is frustration preventing me from succeeding?

Be honest with yourself when trying to determine why you're stumbling; once you've identified the problem(s), brainstorm solutions.

Goal setting is a process that continues over a lifetime. As you grow and change, your goals may change too, and this is fine. You may discover that what you originally wanted to achieve isn't as interesting as you thought. Or you might find that to reach an important goal, you have to give up others along the way. Be flexible yet persistent. Above all, don't give up!

Take Action

Make it a habit to set goals and review them—*daily,* if possible. This may sound difficult, but it's the best way to make goal setting (and goal reaching) a part of your life.

List your long-range and short-range goals and your target dates. Keep notes about your action plan, ways to stay on track, and your successes/setbacks. Write down resources you need, people who can help you, new ideas, problems and solutions, and anything else that relates to your goals. Keep all of this information in one easy-to-find place (a journal is best), so your goals are always "within reach."

You can even write encouraging messages to yourself or inspirational quotes from people you admire; place these sayings where you'll see them daily (like your bedroom mirror or inside your school locker). They'll remind you to keep aiming for your goals each day.

#5 Visualize Your Dreams

Any great accomplishment begins with a vision. A new computer program, a business, a Top Ten song, a blockbuster movie—someone imagined these things before they became real. Creating a mental image of your goals and dreams is a great way to make them happen. Mental imagery, or visualization, helps focus your energy toward success.

Your mind is an amazing tool—and it's up to you to use it well. Your *thoughts* influence how you *feel* and *act.* So when you take charge of your thoughts, you're more in control of your emotions and behaviors. For example, think of an event that might typically make you nervous—like trying out for a sports team. Now imagine the scene: You go to tryouts and see all the other players showing off their skills . . . what happens next?

You might imagine the worst: falling on your face, dropping the ball, or missing every catch. As this scene unfolds in your mind, how does your body react? Your heart probably starts to race, your palms might get sweaty, and you might even feel panicky. If you actually were at tryouts, your nervousness would probably affect your ability to perform.

Now consider this: If you can imagine the worst, you can also imagine the best! Why not use the power of your mind to picture a scenario that makes you feel confident instead of anxious? This is where visualization comes into play.

Athletes often visualize, especially if they're injured and want to mentally practice their sport while sitting on the sidelines. Many athletes also incorporate visualization into their training routine to give themselves a mental edge. Some use it just prior to competing or performing to help reach a state of relaxed readiness. They picture themselves perfectly executing a move, scoring a point, winning a game, or facing an opponent with confidence.

For example, imagine a high jumper before she attempts to clear the bar. She stands motionless, completely focused on the obstacle in front of her. If you could look into her mind as she visualizes, you'd see her envisioning her approach, feeling each foot hit its mark, counting off steps until she launches her body into the air, and arching gracefully over the bar.

You too can use visualization as a tool to help you succeed. Mental imagery gives you the opportunity to rehearse exactly how you want to handle a situation, so you're ready when it happens.

Visualization also enables you to:

- be more calm about situations that make you nervous (tryouts, performances, contests, tests)

- clearly envision your goals and stay committed to them

- be prepared for any challenge

Here's another way to look at visualization: It's kind of like a movie where you're not only the star, but the writer and director, too. You get to develop each scene and plot out a strategy that leads to the ultimate finale—your success.

Take Action

If you can see the goal, you can make it happen. Start with a relaxation exercise so you feel calm and centered. To do this, sit comfortably with your eyes closed. Take a long, slow, deep breath through your nose, counting to five as you inhale. Now breathe out through your nose, slowly counting backwards from five as you exhale. Repeat this rhythmic breathing for about five minutes.

Now you're ready to visualize. Imagine yourself facing a challenge or reaching a goal. Picture each step you need to take and visualize yourself succeeding. Stay relaxed; feel your confidence growing. Use this technique as often as you'd like (you may want to write about it in your journal).

#6 Show Courage

People often think of courage as the absence of fear. True . . . courage means bravery, guts, boldness, daring. But it also means *acting from the heart*. In her book, *Embracing Victory*, author Mariah Burton Nelson wrote: "Courage doesn't mean you're not afraid. Courage is evident when you're afraid and act from the heart anyway."

It's totally normal to feel scared when trying something new or different. Who doesn't get at least a little frightened when facing the unknown? If you confront your fears and move forward in spite of them, you demonstrate courage. You prove to yourself and the world that you're willing to take a risk for something you care about. (NOTE: There's a big difference between *taking a risk* and *putting yourself at risk*. Negative risks, like crazy stunts or harmful behaviors, put you in danger. Positive risks, like getting involved in a new activity or expressing yourself creatively through music, dance, or art, help you stretch yourself and grow. Recognizing the difference between good and bad risks is the first step in keeping safe while trying new things.)

The next time you want to take a healthy risk and you need to summon your courage, remember to do two things: (1) believe in yourself, and (2) think positive. If you're confident that you can handle yourself, and you have faith that things will turn out for the best, you'll be in a better position to face your fears.

But what if you still have butterflies in your stomach? Does this mean you don't have the courage you need? Not necessarily. A rapid heartbeat, heightened awareness, sweaty palms, a rush of adrenaline, and other physical reactions are all part of the human body's *fight-or-flight response.* This is your body's way of getting you ready to go into battle (fight) or run like the wind (flight).

It's up to you to decide whether to fight or flee. To determine whether you're putting yourself in too much physical danger, pay attention to your thinking. If those stomach butterflies are accompanied by thoughts like "This is a bad idea" or "That hill is a lot steeper than I thought!" *listen to them.* Your brain may be sending warning signals that you're about to do something stupid or dangerous. Sometimes courage is thinking twice about a situation and deciding it *isn't* worth the risk.

Every day, people demonstrate remarkable acts of courage. It takes guts to run a marathon, jump out of an airplane, or climb a mountain; and it takes guts to battle an illness, express an opinion, or stand up for a friend. Whether the risks are physical, mental, or both, they require bravery.

Showing courage will help you:

- take healthy risks

- do something you believe in, even if it's difficult

- persist despite setbacks

You need courage to set off on an adventure or forge a new path. You need courage to fulfill your dreams, imagine your success, learn from your mistakes, and keep thinking positively no matter what happens. Most of all, you need courage to learn and grow.

Take Action

Research someone you admire—someone who has faced a fear, demonstrated courage, or been celebrated for heroism (you can read a biography, an autobiography, or a magazine profile, or browse a Web site). What can you learn from this person? What can you do to show similar bravery?

Next, think of something you've been wanting to do but haven't had the courage to try. Then write about what's holding you back. Or write about your biggest fears in general and how they've influenced your life. How can you face them? How can you overcome them?

#7 Be Determined

No matter what you do in life, obstacles (expected or unexpected, large or small) are bound to arise. Life is full of roadblocks, potholes, bumps, hurdles, barriers, and pitfalls. The secret to success is to face each potential obstacle with determination to overcome it.

Being determined means you:

- accept your mistakes and learn from them
- stand strong physically, mentally, and emotionally
- cope with adversity in positive, healthy ways

Determination is a firmness of purpose—it helps you stay focused on your goals. When you really want something, hurdles aren't an excuse to call it quits. If this were the case, sprinter-hurdler Gail Devers never would have stepped back onto the track after complications from a thyroid disorder called Graves' disease nearly resulted in the amputation of her feet. She fought her illness, determined not to let it beat her, and won Olympic gold medals in 1992 and 1996.

You have the power to decide you're not going to let anyone—or anything—come between you and your goals. You may run into obstacles, but they can teach valuable lessons, if you let them. In fact, a hurdle may be a stepping stone on your journey, but only if you face it, overcome it, and learn from it.

The next time you stumble, remember that the true test of determination is how well you bounce back after a letdown. If you get on your feet again, and stay on course, nothing can stop you. As World Champion figure skater Michelle Kwan put it: "To me a champion isn't someone who never loses or falls down. It's someone who gets back up. Someone who has heart."

Take Action

Think of a woman you know and admire—a relative, role model, teacher, mentor, or member of your community. Ask her to share her successes and mistakes, and see what you can learn about her real-life experiences. Write in your journal about the conversation.

For fun, get some crayons or colorful markers and turn to a new page in your journal (or you can do this activity on posterboard). Draw a big, red heart and fill it with things that make you feel happy, proud, and determined to succeed—whatever makes your heart soar! You can write words like "sports," "drama," or "my dream of going to the Caribbean"; or you can draw pictures representing these things. Glue on souvenirs from memorable events (a ticket stub from a movie, a ribbon you won for a school athletic contest, a shell from the beach). Add new items to your heart as often as you wish.

Go Exploring

Any Girl Can Rule the World by Susan M. Brooks (Minneapolis: Fairview Press, 1998). This book is filled with ideas about how young women can feel good about themselves, claim their voices, and make a difference. You'll learn how to publish a 'zine, produce your own cable TV show, and share your opinions with the world.

The Girls' Guide to Life: How to Take Charge of the Issues That Affect You by Catherine Dee (Boston: Little, Brown and Company, 1997). This guide to figuring out life includes ideas on how to raise your self-esteem, feel confident, become successful, and develop a winning attitude.

Girls Who Rocked the World: Heroines from Sacagawea to Sheryl Swoopes by Amelie Welden, illustrated by Jerry McCann (Hillsboro, OR: Beyond Words Publishing, 1998). Read true stories of 33 incredible teen girls, past and present, who have accomplished amazing things in their lives.

Club Girl Tech
http://www.girltech.com
Girl Tech's goal is to raise girls' awareness of and confidence in using technology through products and services created just for them. Visit this site to learn more about inventors, athletes, and adventurers—all of whom are girls and women. Check out the chat rooms, book and movie reviews, celebrity interviews, games, "girl-powered" search engine, and other fun stuff.

Girl Power! Campaign Headquarters
http://www.health.org/gpower/
Girl Power! is the national campaign sponsored by the U.S. Department of Health and Human Services to help encourage and empower girls to make positive choices. Log on to this site for helpful tips on how to increase your *Girl Power!*, ways to feel better about yourself, sports and fitness information, lists of books for girls, and much more. They're always adding more fun stuff, so keep checking in to see what's new.

A Girl's World Online Clubhouse
http://www.agirlsworld.com
This Web site is the space where "girls rule the web!" The site changes regularly, so log on often and check out what's new. You'll find strange-but-true facts, career adventures, chat rooms, entertainment news, sports stories, games, projects, book recommendations, and more.

gURL

http://www.gurl.com

This Web 'zine deals with teen issues in a frank, direct way. It covers topics such as women's history, body image, personal changes, and self-esteem. You'll also find interactive games and chat rooms.

Planet Girl

http://www.planetgirl.com

Planet Girl is an online meeting place for girls to chat, exchange messages, play games, and discover technology. The site is also home to a weekly serial featuring cool characters who are, of course, girls.

Troom

http://www.troom.com/

Sponsored by Tampax, this site features interviews with inspiring female athletes, a page where you can find out answers to whatever questions may be on your mind, girl-specific health information, an advice column, a pen-pal club, quizzes and trivia, links to other sites for girls, and lots more.

Getting Your Body in Shape

What does it mean to get your body in shape? Diet till you look like a toothpick? *(Never!)* Exercise till you drop? *(Of course not!)* Become obsessed with your body and looks? *(No way!)* Your body is the tool that allows you to run, bend, jump, lift, climb, and perform all sorts of other moves, so learn to treat it well.

In "Getting Your Body in Shape," you'll find five tips for taking good care of yourself now and for the rest of your life: (1) be active, (2) avoid injury, (3) eat right, (4) have a positive body image, and (5) stay safe. You might want to use a special journal for the activities included in the "Take Action" exercises.

#1 Be Active

Exercise is good for your body *and* your mind. When you exercise regularly, you increase your fitness level and sharpen your concentration and memory, making you feel healthier from head to toe. Starting an exercise program when you're in your teens (or younger) is the best way to stay fit for a lifetime.

Regular exercise helps you:

- strengthen your heart, lungs, muscles, and bones

- improve muscle tone and reduce body fat

- build up your immune system (allowing you to fight illness better)

- maintain a weight that's right for your body

- decrease your risk of heart disease, high blood pressure, and some forms of cancer later in life

- reduce stress and feelings of depression

- feel good about your body

If you aren't exercising regularly, now's a good time to start!

Where do you begin? Talk to someone who knows about fitness—your doctor, coach, or gym teacher, for example. Get advice about an exercise program that suits your needs. If you currently don't exercise at all, it's best to start slow—don't try to do too much too fast. Work out for ten minutes several times per week. Gradually increase your amount of exercise as you get stronger and more fit, aiming to work out for thirty to forty-five minutes at least three times a week.

If you're currently in good shape, ask yourself if your exercise routine includes the three components of fitness: endurance, strength, and flexibility. Each one plays an important role in your overall health.

Endurance refers to the "staying power" of your heart and lungs. When your heart and lungs are fit, they're able to work efficiently to supply your muscles with oxygen-rich blood, and you don't get as winded during your workouts or day-to-day routine. To improve your endurance, do *aerobic* activities, which use the large muscles (the legs and torso) continuously for at least fifteen minutes. Examples include walking, jogging, biking, in-line skating, and dancing.

Your *strength* is a measure of how much power your muscles have (for example, specific muscles in your upper arms, calves, stomach, or thighs). When your muscles are toned and strong, you're better able to meet physical demands like climbing a challenging rock wall, hitting a punching bag, doing sit-ups, or kicking a ball. Being strong helps protect you from injuries because well-trained muscles are less likely to get overworked or strained. To improve your strength, you can do exercises like push-ups, pull-ups, squats, and lunges or lift weights (be sure to talk to a qualified instructor or coach before trying weight lifting).

Flexibility refers to how limber and elastic your muscles are. When your body is flexible, you reach and bend with ease. You can improve your flexibility by stretching regularly. Make sure your stretching routine involves gentle, sustained stretches—this means bending to the point where you feel comfortable and holding the position for about thirty seconds without bouncing. Release the stretch, then repeat it several times, breathing slowly and easing your body into each new movement.

How much exercise is enough? It depends on your goals. If your goal is to get in shape so you can be active without huffing and puffing, exercise at a moderate level for at least twenty minutes three days a week. To advance your workout, increase the frequency of your activity (to five times a week), the amount of time you spend on it (aim for thirty to forty-five minutes), or both.

You have many options when it comes to exercise. You can do aerobics, play team sports, take a yoga class, try an extreme sport, walk your dog, ride your bike, lift weights, or swim (or all of the above). The most important thing to remember is to HAVE FUN! Choose activities you love, so you look forward to doing them. This is the key to success.

Take Action

If you're ready to begin an exercise program, or to make changes to your existing one, ask yourself the following questions and write down your answers in your journal. This will help you figure out what you want to do and how to get started.

- Which fitness activities sound fun and exciting?

- How much time do you have?

- What resources are available to you (YWCA/YMCA classes, a local recreation center, parks, a pool, hiking trails, school facilities, a dance studio, coaches or gym teachers)?

- What's your budget?

- Is there a friend or other person who may want to join you?

Your goal should be to find several activities you enjoy, so you have a well-rounded exercise plan. If you stick with them and keep adding new ones, you'll be on your way to a lifetime of fun and fitness.

#2 Avoid Injury

No matter what type of workout you do, it's important to warm up your body before you get started. Warming up helps the blood flow through your muscles, making them more limber. When your muscles are limber, they're less likely to become injured. (TIP: Doing a warm-up also gives you time to mentally prepare yourself for the physical challenges of your workout.)

How should you warm up? Simply perform a slower, gentler version of the movements in your activity. For example, if you do aerobics, you can march in place or do basic dance steps for a few minutes. If you swim, you can move around in the pool before doing your laps. After five to ten minutes of movement, your muscles should be warmed up and ready for the next step: stretching.

Stretching further loosens your muscles, making them more elastic and less likely to get pulled or strained. Slowly stretch your neck, arms, torso, and legs. Hold each stretch for fifteen to thirty seconds, pulling gently but not jerking or bouncing. Spend a little extra time stretching muscles that feel especially tight. It's helpful to stretch *after* your workout, too, instead of stopping suddenly. Slowly decreasing your pace, cooling down, and stretching again gives your muscles a chance to recover.

If you've just started a new sport or exercise program, or you've increased the intensity of your current routine, you might feel sore—even if you regularly warm up, stretch, cool down, and stretch some more. A little muscle soreness after a workout is normal.

To relieve the discomfort of minor post-exercise pain, try gently stretching the muscles that hurt. If you want, soak in a warm tub or put ice cubes in a small plastic bag and place them on your sore muscles for about ten minutes.

Don't assume you have to stop exercising until you feel better—working out despite minor soreness is fine. Just be sure to spend extra time warming up, and don't exercise at a high level of intensity. In fact, you might find that exercise helps your sore muscles feel better!

If your discomfort lasts more than seventy-two hours, you may have a sports injury such as a pulled or strained muscle, or something more serious. See a doctor immediately if you experience any of the following symptoms:

- sharp pain, especially with movement
- visible swelling or discoloration
- an inability to put weight or pressure on the affected area
- soreness or pain that doesn't go away in two or three days

Don't assume that all you need is a little rest and ice!

One last thing: *Listen to your body when you exercise.* If your legs or knees are sore when you work out, something might be wrong; talk to a doctor, your parents, your school nurse (if you have one), a gym teacher, or your coach. If your feet hurt, you might need more comfortable athletic shoes, or ones that offer better support. And if working out hurts, STOP. You may be injured or performing the exercise incorrectly; talk to someone who can give you accurate advice about what you need to do.

Physical activity should feel good. The benefits far outweigh the frustrations, so make a commitment to stick with your routine. Stay in tune with your body—let it tell you what's working and what's not.

Take Action

Keep an exercise journal so you have a record of your fitness goals and progress, and the changes you're seeing in your body. If you'd like, write the days of the week in your journal and note the days you work out. Describe how you feel before and after exercising. Note any soreness or injuries, and any positive results. This is an excellent tool for keeping track of your health.

Here are a few more idea-starters for your exercise journal:

- Fitness goal #1:   Target date for reaching it:

- Fitness goal #2:   Target date for reaching it:

- Fitness goal #3:   Target date for reaching it:

- Did you reach your goal(s)? Why or why not?

- Sports or activities you've always wanted to try:

- What's stopping you from trying them:

- Ideas for giving this sport/activity a shot:

- Changes you've noticed in your strength, endurance, and flexibility:

- Ways to stay motivated:

#3 Eat Right

Exercise helps you feel energetic, alert, and ready to tackle the challenges in your life. And so does *eating right.* In fact, eating right and exercising go hand in hand: They're your two best tools for staying healthy and fit all your life.

Because the teen years are a time of change and rapid development, your body needs the right amount of vitamins, minerals, and calories to grow properly. The foods you eat play a major role in keeping you healthy now and as you get older. Eating a balanced diet of nutritious foods shows you care about your body, respect it, and want to take care of it.

Other benefits of good nutrition include:

- healthier bones, muscles, and vital organs (heart, lungs, kidneys)

- a stronger immune system (allowing you to fight illness better)

- a decreased risk of heart disease, high blood pressure, and some forms of cancer later in life

- shinier hair, stronger nails, a better complexion, and healthier gums and teeth

What does it mean to eat right? Having a *balanced* diet—not being on a diet. When you're on a diet, you restrict your food intake and count every calorie; the focus isn't on eating nourishing foods. Most diets are nothing more than empty promises: You skip meals hoping to lose weight, but your body knows you're starving it and goes into "survival mode," hoarding calories and making it harder for you to burn them off.

When you diet, you rob your body of vitamins and minerals and put your health in danger. If you're dieting, STOP. Below, read about how to eat healthy and make good nutrition a part of your life. If you're worried about your weight or if you have a problem with eating, talk to your parents, doctor, or school counselor or to another trusted adult who can help.

Eating right is easy if you follow the Dietary Guidelines created by the United States Department of Health and Human Services (USDHHS). The guidelines consist of seven tips that are simple enough to follow each day:

1. Eat a variety of foods. Learn about what types of foods to eat by looking at the United States Department of Agriculture (USDA) Food Guide Pyramid on the next page.

2. Maintain a healthy weight, and balance the foods you eat with physical activity. How much you should weigh depends on your age, height, frame size, level of activity, heredity, and other factors. The best way to keep your weight within a healthy range is to make a commitment to an active lifestyle and nutritious diet.

3. Eat plenty of fruits, vegetables, and grain products. These foods contain vitamins, minerals, and fiber, all of which your body needs for good health. See the pyramid on the next page for information on how many servings to consume each day.

4. Choose foods that are low in fat and cholesterol. Foods high in fat and cholesterol don't offer vitamins and minerals and shouldn't be a staple of your diet. Consume fatty foods in moderation.

5. Use sugar in moderation. Cut down on sweets such as candy, sodas, cookies, sugary fruit drinks, and doughnuts.

6. Use salt and sodium in moderation. To keep your sodium intake low, eat fewer fast foods and processed foods (like pre-packaged meals, frozen pizzas, chips, etc.). Instead of using lots of table salt, flavor your food with pepper or fresh herbs.

7. If you ever drink alcoholic beverages, do so only in moderation. This recommendation is for adults. If you haven't reached the legal drinking age yet, you shouldn't consume alcohol at all.

The Food Guide Pyramid

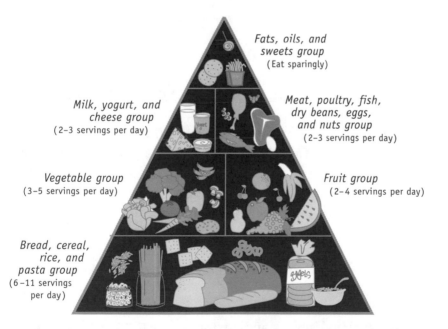

From *Gutsy Girls: Young Women Who Dare* by Tina Schwager, P.T.A., A.T.,C., and Michele Schuerger, © 1999. Free Spirit Publishing Inc., Minneapolis, MN; 800/735/7323. The Food Guide Pyramid may be photocopied for individual or small group use only.

Start with the pyramid, take good care of your body, use your common sense, and talk to your doctor or a nutritionist if you have any questions. You are what you eat, and you'll be much healthier if you give your body what it needs to grow and develop properly.

Take Action

You can get more information about the Dietary Guidelines by writing or calling the Center for Nutrition Policy and Promotion, 1120 20th Street NW, Suite 200, North Lobby, Washington, D.C. 20036; (202) 418-2312. If you're online, you'll find the guidelines at the National Agricultural Library Web site: *http://www.nal.usda.gov/*

To get in touch with the USDA and learn more about the Food Guide Pyramid, write or call the U.S. Department of Agriculture, Washington, D.C. 20250; (202) 720-2791.

You can photocopy the pyramid on page 231 and tape it into your journal. Think about what you eat each day and see if you're getting adequate amounts of fruits, vegetables, dairy products, and other important foods. You can also hang the pyramid on your refrigerator. This will give you—and everyone in your family—an at-a-glance view of what to eat each day.

#4 Have a Positive Body Image

How you feel about your body and appearance is what's called your *body image.* If you look in the mirror and proudly smile at your reflection, you have a positive body image. But if you tend to peer in the mirror and pick out every flaw (real or imagined), you probably have a negative body image. This can adversely affect many areas of your life, including your friendships, schoolwork, and relationships with your family.

There's no such thing as a "perfect" body or looks. If you're trying to live up to an unrealistic image—like pictures of models and movie stars you see in magazines and on billboards—you're setting an impossible standard for yourself. To enhance their looks, models and celebrities have the benefit of makeup and lighting artists, hairstylists, and wardrobe experts (not to mention computer "wizards" who can erase any flaws before the photographs are printed).

If you expect to look like people you see on the pages of fashion magazines, give yourself a break: Why not accept yourself as you are and celebrate your good points instead? Maybe you have your mom's eyes, a great smile, strong hands, or nice calves—these personal traits help make you *you*. You must have at least one or two features that you like; focus on these positive qualities instead of dwelling on what you don't like. Learning to take pride in your unique characteristics is a great way to boost your body image.

It's normal to be self-conscious about your looks once in a while (everyone is sometimes). But an obsession with your appearance can interfere with your day-to-day life. Instead of focusing on what you want to accomplish, you worry about your hair, makeup, clothing, or body size. Remember, your true value lies in your inner qualities, not your looks.

What matters most is what's on the *inside*. You are much more than your appearance: You're someone with unique talents, skills, hopes, and dreams. When you learn to feel good about who you are inside, you'll become more comfortable with who you are on the outside. Learn to be positive, self-assured, goal-oriented, and fun. Other people will naturally be attracted to you.

Take Action

Being physically active is the best way to feel positive about your body, so stick with your commitment to stay in shape. You may even want to have a parent or friend take photos of you playing softball, cheerleading, or doing whatever activity you most enjoy. These pictures can remind you of how good it feels to be active and take pride in your physical health. Keep the photos in your journal, if you'd like.

In your journal, write down five things you like about your body and looks—anything from the color of your hair to the shape of your feet. If you can't think of five things, ask a friend for help. Add to the list as often as possible.

If you still need a boost in the body-image department, here's a tip: Find something you're good at—something you really enjoy. When you're involved in sports or extracurricular activities, it's easier to focus on *what you do* instead of *how you look*. For example, if you consider yourself a good basketball player, singer, student, or youth counselor, your identity is based on your skills rather than your appearance. This can help make you feel more positive about yourself, inside and out.

#5 Stay Safe

Anytime you allow yourself to be creative, express your individuality, or try something new, you take a risk. Being *prepared* will help make it a healthy risk.

No matter what you decide to do—travel, learn to ski, apply for an internship, study abroad, join a team, or whatever—find out ahead of time what to expect. Do you need special knowledge, skills, training, or equipment? What precautions should you take? Who can teach you what you need to learn?

If you decide to "take it to the extreme" by getting involved in a difficult sport or activity, make sure you're ready both physically and mentally. Never use extreme sports as a starting point for getting in shape; these challenges are for serious athletes who are physically fit and have been trained under the supervision of an expert.

If you're planning to try an extreme sport or an adventure, be sure to hook up with a qualified professional or organization. Ask the guides or instructors to show you their credentials. You may want to attend a training center or camp to get in-depth instruction from certified coaches or teachers.

Most extreme sports or adventures have different levels, from beginner to advanced to pro. Ask your instructor, equipment outfitter, or organization chapter for more information about any qualifying tests you need to take. You may have to start with the basics, but this helps ensure your safety. With practice and experience, you'll be able to advance to more challenging levels.

Before setting off on a difficult travel adventure, be sure you're equipped to handle the demands of the journey. Start with a smaller trip to determine if you enjoy being away from home, meeting new people, enduring harsh climates, and going without the comforts you may be accustomed to at home. Spend time educating yourself about the places you want to go and any potential dangers that await. Being informed will help you avoid unwanted surprises.

Once you've signed up for an adventure or outing, find out if you need special equipment or clothing. Learn about the climate, terrain, wildlife, sleeping arrangements, and any precautions regarding food or water.

Whether you head off on an adventure or get involved in an extreme sport, be sure to use the recommended safety gear—no exceptions! You may need to purchase special shoes, insulated clothing, wrist (or elbow or knee) pads, a life jacket, a helmet, goggles, or a first-aid kit. Find out what's required, buy or rent it, and *use it.*

Take Action

To learn more about adventures, daring sports, or similar challenges, you can read books and magazines, contact national organizations, check out Web sites, or talk to people who can provide insight and advice (you'll find lots of resources in the "Go Exploring" sections throughout this book). You can also participate in classes or seminars offered by local clubs, sporting shops, or schools. For example, many community colleges and universities hold extension classes designed to introduce people to sports or travel adventures. Gyms, youth centers, community centers, or your local YWCA/YMCA may have training programs, too. Learn all you can, so you're ready for anything. Keep notes about your findings in your journal.

To push yourself beyond your comfort zone takes guts. It also takes a strong body, sharp mind, and willing spirit. In the words of author Martha Grimes: "We don't know who we are until we see what we can do." Are you ready to see what you can do?

Go Exploring

The Right Moves: A Girl's Guide to Getting Fit and Feeling Good by Tina Schwager, P.T.A., A.T.,C., and Michele Schuerger (Minneapolis: Free Spirit Publishing Inc., 1998). What does it take to be totally fit inside and out? It's a blend of attitude, eating right, and exercise, and this book covers all three topics. You'll find out how to boost your self-esteem; find a fitness plan that's right for you; eat right at home, at school, and even at the mall; and take good care of yourself from head to toe.

Women's Sports & Fitness
P.O. Box 50034
Boulder, CO 80323
1-800-274-0084
http://www.condenast.com

This women's fitness magazine includes features profiling athletes, training tips, nutrition, and general fitness-related stories. Pro beach volleyball player, Gabrielle Reece, writes a monthly column.

Go, girl! Magazine
http://www.gogirlmag.com
Go, girl! is a Web site dedicated to inspiring girls and women to get involved in sports for the fun and joy of it—no matter what their age or fitness level. You'll find fitness news, profiles of women involved in sports or fitness, links to other sites, and much more.

Nike Girls in the Game
http://www.nike.com/girls/
This site—by and for girl athletes—offers personal stories and opinions of what it's like to be athletic. Read what female team members say about how it feels to be involved in sports.

Girls, Inc.
120 Wall Street, 3rd Floor
New York, NY 10005
(212) 509-2000
http://www.girlsinc.org

The goal of this organization is to make sports an important part of girls' lives. Girls ages 6–18 learn basic sports skills, various team and individual sports, and the value of teamwork. The programs are run by female coaches and role models.

Kids In Sports
Girls Coordinator
3990 South Menlo Avenue, 2nd Floor
Los Angeles, CA 90037
(213) 765-1900
The goal of Kids In Sports is to introduce athletics to girls 8–14 who might not otherwise have the chance to participate. Girls can participate in basketball, baseball, softball, volleyball, swimming, and soccer competitions.

National Association for Girls and Women in Sport (NAGWS)
1900 Association Drive
Reston, VA 20191
(703) 476-3450
http://www.aahperd.org/nagws/nagws.html
NAGWS is committed to getting girls and women involved in physical activity and sports, as both participants and leaders. The organization helps coordinate the annual National Girls and Women in Sports Day (this day, created in honor of volleyball player Flo Hyman, celebrates women athletes and their struggle for equality in sports). The organization also develops sports programs for athletes of all ages and abilities, holds conferences, and publishes newsletters and journals to educate members about professional opportunities.

The President's Council on Physical Fitness and Sports
Department of Health and Human Services
Hubert H. Humphrey Bldg., Room 738H
200 Independence Avenue SW
Washington, D.C. 20201
(202) 690-9000
The President's Council is dedicated to getting Americans of all ages more involved in sports and physical fitness. With the main focus being the youth of America, the council sponsors fitness challenges in schools to promote early involvement in physical activity. The goal is to get kids active so they will grow up to be healthier adults.

Women's Sports Foundation
Eisenhower Park
East Meadow, NY 11554
1-800-227-3988
http://www.lifetimetv.com/WoSport
This nonprofit foundation supports and encourages women's participation in sports through awards, grants, scholarships, research, and education. The Web site provides information about various sports, organizations, legal issues, and scholarship applications.

Gutsy Women (and Girls) Who Made History

 ## Auto Racing

1909—The Women's Motoring Club holds the first all-female auto race, from New York City to Philadelphia and back.

1910—Blanche Stuart Scott, 19, begins the first solo auto trip across the country by a female driver. On September 2, 1910, she becomes the first American female to fly solo in an airplane.

1965—Shirley Muldowney is the first woman licensed by the National Hot Rod Association (NHRA) to drive a top-gas dragster. In 1977, she becomes the first woman to drive ¼ mile in under 6 seconds. In 1977, '80, and '82, she wins the NHRA's Top Fuel Winston World Championship. She goes on to win 17 NHRA titles.

1975—Karren Stead, 11, becomes the first girl to win the All-American Soap Box Derby.

1976—Kitty O'Neil sets the women's land speed record of 612 mph.

1977—Janet Guthrie, a 39-year-old physicist, is the first woman to compete in the Indy 500.

1985—Lyn St. James places first at the Watkins Glen International race track in New York, becoming the first woman to win a solo North American professional road race. That year, she also becomes the first woman to average more than 200 mph on an oval track (Talladega Superspeedway, Alabama).

1988—Shawna Robinson becomes the first woman to win a major National Association for Stock Car Auto Racing (NASCAR) event, the AC Delco 100 NASCAR race, Dash division.

1992—Lyn St. James is the second woman to qualify for the Indy 500, where she finishes eleventh, and becomes the first female Indy 500 Rookie of the Year.

1994—Shawna Robinson wins the pole position (the inside front row position on the starting line) at the Busch Light 300, the first time in history a woman has earned this position at a Grand National NASCAR race.

1997—Cristen Powell wins the Mopar Parts Nationals in Englishtown, New Jersey, to become the youngest woman to win a national event in Top Fuel.

Aviation

1911—Harriet Quimby becomes the first American licensed female pilot in the United States. In 1912, she is the first woman to fly across the English Channel, and the first female pilot authorized to fly U.S. mail.

1921—Bessie Coleman becomes the first African-American woman to earn an international pilot's license.

1928—Amelia Earhart is the first woman to cross the Atlantic ocean by plane (she is a passenger, not the pilot).

1930—Ruth Nichols breaks the women's east-west transcontinental speed record and turns around and breaks the west-east flying record.

1932—Marian Cummings is the first woman to receive a commercial pilot's license.

—Amelia Earhart, in a Lockheed Vega monoplane, begins the first solo flight across the Atlantic by a woman.

1937—Willa Brown is the first African-American commercial airline pilot.

—Amelia Earhart disappears somewhere over the Pacific Ocean during her attempt to fly around the world.

1953—Jacqueline Cochran, while flying, is the first woman to break the sound barrier.

1973—Bonnie Tiburzi becomes the first woman hired as a jet pilot by a major U.S. airline (flying a Boeing 727 for American Airlines).

1986—Jeana Yeager and Dick Rutan, in the aircraft *Voyager,* are the first pilots to fly around the world without stopping or refueling.

1991—Patty Wagstaff is the first woman to win the U.S. National Aerobatic Championship. She wins again in 1992 and 1993.

1994—Merce Marti, flying in a general aviation airplane, is the first woman pilot to win the Race Around the World.

—Vicki Van Meter, 12, is the youngest person to fly across the Atlantic Ocean from Augusta, Maine, to Glasgow, Scotland.

1996—Jessica Dubroff, 7, dies during takeoff in a rainstorm while trying to become the youngest person ever to fly coast-to-coast across the U.S.

Climbing

1906—Fanny Bullock Workman sets the world climbing record for women (23,300 feet) by reaching the top of Pinnacle Peak in Nun Kun Massif in Kashmir (located north of India and Pakistan), a record that stands until 1934. She is also one of the first women to climb the Matterhorn, in Switzerland, and Mont Blanc, Europe's highest mountain.

1908—Annie Smith Peck climbs Huascarán, the highest mountain in Peru (21,812 feet).

1911—Annie Smith Peck conquers the 21,079 foot north summit of Mount Coropuna, also in Peru.

1947—Barbara Washburn is the first woman to reach the summit of Alaska's Mount McKinley (along with her husband, Bradford).

1970—Arlene Blum organizes and takes part in the first all-female expedition to the summit of Mount McKinley.

1975—Junko Tabei of Japan becomes the first woman to reach the top of Mount Everest.

1978—An all-female team, led by Arlene Blum, climbs Annapurna in the Himalayas, the tenth highest peak in the world. Thirteen women begin the expedition, and two die along the way.

1980—Lynn Hill climbs Ophir Broke in Telluride, Colorado, the first woman to make the ascent.

1990—Lynn Hill is the first woman to complete a grade 5.14 climb (a high level of difficulty), in Cimai, France.

1992–1995—Robyn Erbesfield is ranked first in the World Cup Championships all four years.

1993—Kitty Calhoun, a high-altitude mountaineer, attempts to climb the north ridge of Latok in Pakistan.

1994—Lynn Hill achieves the previously considered "impossible feat" of free-climbing the "Nose" route on El Capitan, in California's Yosemite National Park.

1995—Merrick Johnston, 12, becomes the youngest person to climb Mount McKinley.

Equestrian Sports

1804—Alicia Meynell of England becomes the first female jockey.

1904—Bertha Kapernick is the first woman to give a bronco riding exhibition.

1911—Nan Jane Aspinwall completes a 3,000 mile solo horseback trip across the United States.

1968—Anne Lewis wins the women's Pro Rodeo Association barrel racing title, the youngest person ever to win a rodeo world championship (at only 10 years of age).

1970—Diane Crump is the first female jockey to ride in the Kentucky Derby.

1991—Julie Krone is the first female jockey to ride in the Belmont Stakes.

1993—Julie Krone is the first female jockey to win a Triple Crown race (riding Colonial Affair in the Belmont Stakes).

Exploration & Discovery

1847—Maria Mitchell, an astronomer, discovers a new comet using a 2 inch telescope. In 1848, she becomes the first woman elected to the American Academy of Arts and Sciences. She goes on to cofound the Association for the Advancement of Women.

1860s—Florence Baker is one of the first Europeans to explore the hidden sources of the Nile (the Nile was a source of life and sustenance for the ancient Egyptians).

1890—Elizabeth Cochrane Seaman, a New York journalist who uses the pen name Nellie Bly, completes her round-the-world trip (traveling on trains, boats, and horses) in a record time of 72 days, 6 hours and 11 minutes. Her time beats the record of fictional hero Phileas Fogg (from Jules Verne's *Around the World in 80 Days*).

1901—Esther Van Deman is the first female Roman field archaeologist.

1905—Nettie Stevens, through her study of meal worms, identifies the X and Y chromosomes, which determine sex.

1912—Juliette Gordon Low founds the Girl Scouts of the U.S.A., the largest voluntary organization for girls. In 1950, the Girl Scouts is reincorporated under a congressional charter. Forty million girls have joined since the organization's inception.

1924—Delia Akeley leads a safari across central Africa to the remote regions of the Belgian Congo. She collects wildlife specimens and lives with Pygmies for several months.

—Disguised as a beggar, Alexandra David-Neel becomes the first woman to travel to the forbidden city of Lhasa, Tibet.

1925—Harriet Chalmers Adams cofounds the Society of Women Geographers and becomes its first president.

1928—Margaret Mead, an anthropologist interested in finding out how culture influences personality, publishes *Coming of Age in Samoa*.

1958—Rachel Carson, a biologist and environmentalist, performs research showing that toxic chemicals poison the earth. In 1962, she publishes *Silent Spring*.

1967—Dian Fossey, a zoologist, travels to Rwanda to study mountain gorillas. In 1983, she publishes *Gorillas in the Mist*.

1977—Rosalyn Yalow is the first American woman to win the Nobel Prize for medicine.

1986—Margaret Joan Geller codiscovers the "Great Wall"—thousands of galaxies arranged across the universe.

—Ann Bancroft is the first woman to travel across the ice to the North Pole.

1988—Gertrude Elion is awarded the Nobel Prize for medicine for her creation of drugs to combat leukemia, gout, malaria, herpes, and autoimmune disorders.

—Helen Thayer is the first woman to travel solo (on foot and on skis) to the North Pole. She is accompanied by her dog, Charlie.

1991—Antonia Novella is the first woman and first Hispanic to be appointed U.S. Surgeon General.

—Bernadine Healy is the first female to head the National Institutes of Health (NIH).

1992—The Autogenic Feedback Training System designed to minimize motion sickness without the use of drugs—developed by NASA research scientist Patricia S. Cowing—is put to use during an 8-day flight of the Space Shuttle *Endeavour*.

1993—U.S. astronomer Carolyn Shoemaker, along with husband Eugene and fellow astronomer David Levy, discover the comet Shoemaker-Levy 9, the team's ninth comet discovery. Shoemaker-Levy 9 crashes into Jupiter in July 1994. Carolyn goes on to discover over 30 comets during her career, more than any other female astronomer.

The Military

1782—Deborah Sampson enlists in the Continental Army as a man (under the name Robert Shirtliffe) and fights in several battles against the British.

1812—Lucy Brewer conceals her gender to become the first female marine. She serves (as George Baker) aboard the USS *Constitution*.

1861—Sarah Emma Edmonds enlists in the Union Army as a man. In 1863, she contracts malaria and deserts the army to avoid detection. After recovering, she returns to the battlefront as a nurse.

1917—Loretta Walsh is the first woman to enlist in the U.S. Navy.

1942—The first group of female pilots flies for the armed forces.

1969—The U.S. Navy admits women to the Antarctic Research Program.

1974—The first women are admitted to the U.S. Merchant Marine Academy.

—Barbara Rainey becomes the first female aviator in the U.S. Navy.

1975—Congress passes a bill authorizing the admission of women to the nation's military academies by fall of 1976.

1977—Janna Lambine becomes the first female U.S. Coast Guard pilot.

1979—Beverly Gwinn Kelley is the first woman to command a U.S. Coast Guard vessel at sea.

1985—Gail Reals is the first woman promoted to rank of brigadier general in the U.S. Marine Corps.

1991—Melissa Rathbun-Nealy is the first U.S. woman POW (prisoner of war) in the regular army.

1994—USS *Eisenhower* is the first Navy combat ship to have women permanently assigned.

1995—Rebecca E. Marier is the first female valedictorian at West Point (the U.S. Military Academy).

—Shannon Faulkner becomes the first female cadet at the Citadel (Military College of South Carolina).

Nontraditional Sports

1876—The first U.S. women's boxing match is held (Nell Saunders defeats Rose Harland).

1901—Anna Edson Taylor becomes the first person to go over Niagara Falls in a barrel and survive.

1913—Georgia Broadwick makes the first parachute jump by a woman.

1937—Doris Kopsky covers 1 mile in 4 minutes, 22.4 seconds to become the first female champion of the National Amateur Bicycle Association.

1966—Joyce Hoffman (an American) wins her second straight surfing championship in Sydney, Australia, becoming the first woman to win this title twice.

1970—Sally Younger, 17, sets the women's speed record on water skis, going 105.14 mph.

—Ringling Bros. and Barnum & Bailey Circus signs Peggy Williams and Maudie Flippen to join the formerly all-male Clown Alley.

1985—Libby Riddles becomes the first woman to win the Iditarod, the 1,135 mile Alaskan dog sled race. She makes it in 18 days.

1990—Cara-Beth Burnside is the first woman to become a professional skateboarder.

1993—Mountain bike racer Juli Furtado is the first woman to be named by *VeloNews: The Journal of Competitive Cycling,* as Cyclist of the Year.

1995—The first-ever Golden Gloves tournament for women is held. Jill Matthews becomes flyweight (the weight class with a maximum weight of 112 pounds) champion.

—Hillary Wolf is the first American ever to win a gold medal in the World Junior Judo Championships.

1997—Tara Hamilton sets a world record for the most points earned by a woman on the wakeboarding pro tour.

1998—Kimarie Hanson is the youngest female to enter and finish the Iditarod.

—Melissa Buhl, during the Bicycle Motocross (BMX) Nationals, becomes the first female to race against male riders at the A Pro level.

The Olympics

1928—Betty Robinson is the first American woman to win an Olympic gold medal in track and field (100 meters).

1948—Alice Coachman is the first black woman, and the only American woman, to win an Olympic gold medal in track and field at the 1948 Olympic Games.

—Gretchen Fraser is the first U.S. athlete to win an Olympic medal in skiing (slalom).

1960—African-American athlete Wilma Rudolph becomes the first American woman to win three gold medals in a single Olympics (in track and field). She is the first American to win both Olympic sprint events and the first American to win an Olympic 200 meter event.

1964—Wyomia Tyus, 18, wins the gold medal in the 100 meters at the Olympics. She wins again four years later, becoming the first Olympian to win consecutive gold medals in any event.

—Three-Day Eventing (Olympic horseback riding) is opened to women.

1976—Women's basketball debuts at the Olympics as a medal sport.

—Nadia Comaneci, 14, of Romania is the first gymnast to receive a perfect score in Olympic competition.

1984—Valerie Brisco is the first athlete to win a gold medal in the 200 and 400 meters in a single Olympics.

—Women participate in cycling events for the first time—and the first U.S. medal is won by Connie Carpenter-Phinney.

—American cyclist Rebecca Twigg finishes second in the first Olympic women's road race event.

—Karen Stives is the first American woman to win an individual medal (silver) in Olympic equestrian competition. She is also a member of the gold medal-winning Three-Day Eventing team.

—Mary Lou Retton becomes the first American to win the Olympic all-around gymnastics title.

1988 & 1992—Nicole Uphoff of West Germany is the only woman ever to win two individual Olympic medals in dressage.

1992—Donna Weinbrecht of the United States wins the gold medal in the first-ever women's Olympic moguls (ungroomed bumps on a ski run) competition.

—Cammy Myler has the best U.S. women's finish ever in Olympic luge competition.

1996—Women's fast pitch softball becomes an Olympic medal sport.

—American women athletes win Olympic gold medals in softball, soccer, basketball, and team gymnastics.

1998—Women's ice hockey debuts at the Olympic Games in Nagano, Japan, and the United States wins the gold.

—Picabo Street wins the Olympic gold medal in downhill skiing after a string of injuries.

Sailing

1969—Sharon Sites Adams is the first woman to complete a solo sail across the Pacific in her 31 foot ketch. She travels 5,620 miles from Yokohama, Japan, to San Diego, California, in 74 days, 17 hours, and 15 minutes.

1985—Tania Aebi, 18, becomes the youngest person to sail around the world, accompanied only by her cats. It took her 2½ years to complete the 27,000 mile journey aboard her 26 foot sloop, *Varuna*.

1994—The first all-female America's Cup team is selected. The team, America³, consisting of 24 women, competes for the first time in the 1995 America's Cup yacht race.

—Isabelle Autissier, along with three crew members, sails from New York harbor, around Cape Horn, to the Golden Gate Bridge in San Francisco in 62 days, 5 hours, and 55 minutes. She is the fourth person to set a new record for this sail, and the first woman to accomplish this feat.

1998—Karen Thorndike is the first American woman to complete a solo circumnavigation of the world in the open ocean and around the five Great Capes—Cape Horn (tip of South America), Cape of Good Hope (South Africa), Cape Leeuwin (south of Perth, Australia), South East Cape (Tasmania), and Southwest Cape (south of New Zealand). She had sailed for just over two years aboard her 36 foot yacht, *Amelia*.

Space Exploration

1978—The first female U.S. astronauts are selected: Anna Fisher, Shannon Lucid, Judith Resnick, Sally Ride, Margaret Seddon, and Kathryn Sullivan.

1983—Sally Ride, 32, begins a 6-day mission aboard the Space Shuttle *Challenger,* becoming the first American woman to travel in space and the youngest American astronaut to circle the earth.

1985—Tamara E. Jernigan, 26, is the youngest U.S. astronaut candidate.

1986—Christa McAuliffe, the first civilian and "Teacher in Space," dies when all seven members of the Space Shuttle *Challenger* are killed in an explosion during liftoff. Judith Resnick, one of the first female astronauts, is also on board.

1992—Dr. Mae Jemison becomes the first African-American woman in space, aboard the Space Shuttle *Endeavour.*

1993—Dr. Ellen Ochoa is the first Hispanic woman in space.

1995—Eileen Collins becomes the first female astronaut to pilot a space mission, aboard the Space Shuttle *Discovery.*

1998—NASA names Eileen Collins as the first female Space Shuttle Commander for a mission aboard the Space Shuttle *Columbia.*

Swimming

1926—Gertrude Ederle becomes the first woman to swim across the English Channel. She swims 35 miles from Cap Gris-Nez, France, to Dover, England, in a time of 14 hours, 39 minutes—almost two hours faster than any man before her. Her hearing is permanently impaired from her effort.

1952—Florence Chadwick is the first woman to swim from Catalina Island to the California mainland.

1973—Lynne Cox of the United States swims from England to France in 9 hours, 36 minutes, the fastest time recorded by a woman.

1975—Diana Nyad is the first woman to swim around Manhattan Island; she is also the first person to swim across Lake Ontario, completing 32 miles in 20 hours.

1979—Sylvia Earle is the first person in the world to dive to 1,250 feet.

—Diana Nyad sets the world record for the longest swim, 102.5 miles.

1994—Lynne Cox completes the "peace swim," swimming 14 miles across the Gulf of 'Aqaba. This accomplishment symbolically united the warring nations of Jordan, Israel, and Egypt.

1997—Susie Maroney is the first person to swim from Cuba to Florida.

1998—Susie Maroney becomes the first person to swim from Mexico to Cuba and sets a world record for the longest nonstop, unassisted open-water swim (128 miles in 38 hours, 27 minutes).

5 Team Sports

1892—Senda Berenson adapts the rules of basketball for women and introduces the game at Smith College in Massachusetts.

1963—Nancy Lotsey becomes the first girl to play in an organized all-boy baseball competition. In her first game, she is the winning pitcher and hits a home run.

1974—Girls are officially admitted to Little League.

1977—Brown University forms the first women's soccer team in the United States.

1979—Ann Meyers is the first woman to sign a National Basketball Association (NBA) contract.

1984—Georgeann Wells, of West Virginia University, is the first woman to dunk during a basketball game.

1985—Lynette Woodard becomes the first female member of the Harlem Globetrotters basketball team.

1986—Nancy Lieberman becomes the first woman to play in a men's professional basketball league.

1987—The first annual National Girls and Women in Sports Day is held (this day, created in honor of volleyball player Flo Hyman, celebrates women athletes and their struggle for equality in sports).

1989—Julie Croteau becomes the first woman to play for a men's National Collegiate Athletic Association (NCAA) baseball team, playing first base for Division III St. Mary's College in St. Mary's City, Maryland.

—Victoria Brucker is the first girl to play for a U.S. team in a Little League World Series game.

1990—Kelly Craig becomes the first girl to start as pitcher in the Little League World Series.

1992—Manon Rheaume is signed by the Atlanta Knights, becoming the first woman ever to play in a professional hockey regular season game.

1994—The first women's professional baseball team, the Colorado Silver Bullets, has its premier season.

—The University of Minnesota opens the Tucker Center, the first research center in the United States to study girls and women in sports.

1996—The American Basketball League (ABL) and the Women's National Basketball Association (WNBA) are formed.

1997—Dee Kantner and Violet Palmer become the first female referees in the NBA.

—2.4 million girls are playing high school sports, an 800 percent increase since 1971.

—Elizabeth Heaston is the first woman to play and score in a college football game.

1998—Pitcher Ila Borders is the first woman to win a men's professional minor league baseball game.

Index

About the Authors

Tina Schwager is a Certified Athletic Trainer (A.T.,C.) and licensed Physical Therapy Assistant (P.T.A.). She earned a B.A. in Athletic Training from California State University. During her 11 years of athletic training, she has worked in the clinical, Olympic, high school, and university levels. Currently, she works for a physical rehabilitation center, developing programs for athletes and celebrities. Tina is committed to a lifestyle of health and fitness, and to helping others achieve their fitness goals. She has 13 years experience as an aerobics instructor, and her "Back In Action" exercise video—which she wrote, produced, and appeared in—is designed to help people strengthen their lower back muscles. Tina is also a public speaker who has toured universities, high schools, and corporations to lecture on topics such as fitness and injury prevention/rehabilitation.

Michele Schuerger holds a B.A. in Communication Studies from the University of California Los Angeles (UCLA). She has worked in the entertainment industry for the past 13 years and is currently employed at an advertising agency. She helped Tina write and produce the "Back In Action" video, and co-starred in the production. Michele's athletic career included 8 years of competitive figure skating, and she continues to enjoy noncompetitive skating and many other types of exercise. She believes that her involvement in sports encouraged her positive attitude, increased her confidence, and helped her find the courage to pursue her dream of writing books.

Tina and Michele published their first book, *The Right Moves: A Girl's Guide to Getting Fit and Feeling Good,* with Free Spirit Publishing in 1998.

OTHER GREAT BOOKS FROM FREE SPIRIT

The Right Moves
A Girl's Guide to Getting Fit and Feeling Good
by Tina Schwager, P.T.A., A.T.,C., and Michele Schuerger
This upbeat guide encourages girls to realize their full potential by developing a healthy self-image, eating right, and becoming physically fit. For ages 11 & up.
$14.95; 280 pp.; softcover; illus.; 7" x 9"

The Kid's Guide to Social Action
How to Solve the Social Problems You Choose—
and Turn Creative Thinking into Positive Action
Revised, Expanded, Updated Edition
by Barbara A. Lewis
This exciting, empowering book includes everything kids need to make a difference in the world: step-by-step directions for writing letters, doing interviews, raising funds, getting media coverage, and more. For ages 10 & up.
$16.95; 224 pp.; softcover; B&W photos and illus.; 8½" x 11"

Making Every Day Count
Daily Readings for Young People on Solving Problems, Setting Goals, & Feeling Good About Yourself
by Pamela Espeland and Elizabeth Verdick
Each entry in this book of daily readings includes a thought-provoking quotation, a brief essay, and a positive "I"-statement that relates the entry to the reader's own life. For ages 11 & up.
$9.95; 392 pp.; softcover; 4¼" x 6¼"

To place an order or to request a free catalog
of SELF–HELP FOR KIDS® and SELF–HELP FOR TEENS® materials,
please write, call, email, or visit our Web site:

Free Spirit Publishing Inc.
400 First Avenue North • Suite 616 • Minneapolis, MN 55401
toll-free 800.735.7323 • local 612.338.2068 • fax 612.337.5050
help4kids@freespirit.com • www.freespirit.com